HIGH ROYDS HOSPITAL

MEDICAL LIBRARY - Ext 6227

Books should be returned by the last date shown
above. Renewal may be made by personal application, in writing or be telephone.
FINES ARE CHARGED FOR OVERDUE
BOOKS.

ASSESSMENT OF MENTAL CAPACITY

GUIDANCE FOR DOCTORS AND LAWYERS

This report outlines the current legal requirements
in England and Wales concerning assessment of
mental capacity. Practical guidelines on the
medical assessment of capacity are included.

First published in 1995

British Library Cataloguing Publication Data
A catalogue record for this book is available from the British Library

ISBN 0 7279 0913 4

Typeset in Great Britain by
DataNet

Membership of the Working Party

James Birley	Psychiatrist, former BMA President
Nigel Eastman	Forensic psychiatrist and barrister (non-practising) Secretary of the Mental Health Law Subcommittee of the Royal College of Psychiatrists and member of the Law Society Mental Health & Disability Committee
J Stuart Horner	Chairman, BMA's Medical Ethics Committee
Penny Letts	Secretary, Law Society Mental Health & Disability Committee
Denzil Lush	Solicitor, member of the Law Society Mental Health & Disability Committee
Lydia Sinclair	Solicitor, member of the Law Society Mental Health & Disability Committee, Mental Health Act Commissioner
Ann Sommerville	BMA Advisor on Medical Ethics
David Watts	General practitioner, member of the BMA's Medical Ethics Committee

Contributing Authors

Nigel Eastman	Member of Working Party
Michael Hinchliffe	Office of the Official Solicitor
Penny Letts	Member of Working Party
Denzil Lush	Member of Working Party
Steven Luttrell	Whittington Hospital
Lydia Sinclair	Member of Working Party
Ann Sommerville	Member of Working Party

Editor	Neil Lambe	King's College, London
Editorial Secretary	Gillian Romano	
Project Manager	Rosemary Weston	

We are grateful to the many organisations and individuals who took the trouble to comment on our first draft.

Contents

PART III LEGAL TESTS OF CAPACITY

PART IV PRACTICAL ASPECTS OF THE ASSESSMENT OF CAPACITY

Table of Cases

PART I

Introduction

1 Introduction and Background

1:1 The need to define capacity

The prime principle which underpins both current law and medical practice with regard to issues of mental capacity is, as the Law Commission for England and Wales (hereafter referred to as the Law Commission) has stated, that people should be "enabled and encouraged to take for themselves those decisions which they are able to take" (Law Commission Report No 231 (1995), para 2.46). Doctors and lawyers have common responsibilities to ensure the protection of people who are incapable of deciding matters for themselves and to promote the choices of those who can and should regulate their own lives. The careful assessment of whether individuals have or lack capacity is essential to the protection of their rights. Effective communication, both between the professionals involved and with the person being assessed is vital. This book sets out to aid communication between doctors and lawyers and clarify the framework within which it takes place.

As advance directives and proxy decision-making attract public attention, general practitioners and family lawyers are increasingly consulted by healthy people wishing to make provision for their future care and medical treatment when capacity is lost. In this and many other areas, doctors and lawyers frequently have to define the notion of capacity in order to ensure that the rights and needs of patients and clients are properly recognised.

Capacity, however, can mean something different to each profession and the manner in which it is assessed also varies. All adults are presumed to have legal capacity unless there is evidence to the contrary (see Part II). The Law Commission has recently carried out a lengthy consultation on the subject of mentally incapacitated adults and has published a draft Bill (Clauses 1-5 of the draft Bill are set out in Appendix A) which defines a person as lacking mental capacity:

"if at the material time-
(a) he is unable by reason of mental disability to make a decision for himself on the matter in question; or
(b) he is unable to communicate his decision on that matter because he is unconscious or for any other reason".

This definition reflects the current legal position that capacity must be assessed in relation to the particular decision the individual purports to make (see Part III).

1:2 How to use this book

This book sets out to provide a useful resource tool for both the health and legal professions. It is intended to be a source of key references appropriate to any assessment of mental capacity. Some repetition in the text is unavoidable and is indeed desirable since it is expected that health and legal professionals will dip into the sections as they are relevant to a particular client rather than read the book from cover to cover. Part II broadly discusses some relevant legal principles as they apply to mental capacity. It provides a general background by explaining the role of the law in relation to assessment of capacity. This material will be familiar to lawyers but may be useful in setting the scene for other professionals. Part III examines the legal tests which apply to various projects an individual may wish to undertake, such as writing a will or getting married. In order for any person to be judged mentally capable of validly undertaking a particular project, he or she must meet standards set by statute or by the courts. Different requirements apply to different decisions. Lawyers often seek medical reports when they are requested to advise or act on behalf of a client whose mental capacity is in doubt. Lawyers who ask doctors to assess a person's capacity should always make clear the nature of the project the person hopes to achieve and the law's requirements for it to be validly undertaken. Part III, by clarifying the minimum legal requirement for a number of projects, is primarily intended as a reminder to lawyers and to help doctors who have been asked to conduct an assessment of a person's capacity. References to statute and case law are given where appropriate.

In some cases, medical practitioners have to assess an individual's mental capacity not in order to inform others but to clarify whether medical treatment can proceed without the patient's consent. Whether an apparent consent or refusal of treatment is legally valid is discussed in the later chapters of Part III, which is aimed primarily at health professionals. Part IV deals with the medical practicalities of assessing capacity. Chapter 12 sets down accepted practice for carrying out assessments of capacity and will be familiar to practitioners who regularly work in the mental health field. It is primarily intended, therefore, to assist health professionals who only occasionally encounter a request for an assessment of capacity to be carried out. Chapter 13 aims to help lawyers direct their requests appropriately and to be aware of the steps involved in a medical assessment.

1:3 Scope of this book

1:3.1 What is covered?

The aims of the book are two-fold. It states the legal position in England and Wales regarding the rights and treatment of people who may or may not lack mental capacity and indicates the relationship between law and accepted medical practice. Reference is included, where relevant, to the recommendations for new legislation published by the Law Commission in March 1995 (see section 1:7), but the law examined here is that currently in force at the time of publication. The book brings together guidance for doctors and lawyers on what is understood by the concept of capacity in various situations. The focus is on civil law. Case studies are provided in Appendix B. The purpose of these examples is to give solicitors and doctors practical guidance (a) on situations in which it may be necessary to assess a person's capacity, (b) on how to assess capacity and (c) highlighting any professional/ethical dilemmas that may arise.

1:3.2 What is not covered?

The book deals only with the legal provisions in England and Wales. It does not deal with other parts of the UK. (The possibility of joint publications between the British Medical Association (BMA) and the Law Society of Scotland and of Northern Ireland is, however, under discussion.) Nor, with two exceptions, does this book look at the law relating to the capacity of children. The exceptions concern the capacity of children to consent to or refuse consent to medical procedures and to research which is dealt with in chapters 10 and 11. Aspects of the criminal law are omitted apart from questions which may arise in the context of personal and sexual relationships which are covered in chapter 9. Therefore issues such as a defendant's "fitness to plead" or the need for an "appropriate adult" to be present during police questioning are not considered. This book also does not consider issues arising from a person's physical incapacity, although it is recognised that it is not always easy to distinguish between physical and mental incapacity, for example when considering the fitness to drive of a person suffering from dementia.

Further, even in relation to the civil law, no consideration is given to those aspects of the Mental Health Act 1983 which relate to detention in hospital or capacity to consent to treatment for mental disorder (as dealt with in Parts II-IV of the Act). Where the 1983 Act applies to a patient, its provisions override the provisions of the common law relating to capacity to consent to treatment. There is, however, an important interface between the common law relating to capacity to consent to medical treatment and the provisions of the 1983 Act which should be made clear. The provisions of that Act are concerned solely with treatment for mental disorder and it is therefore not possible to use those provisions in order to undertake any surgical or other medical procedures which are unrelated to the patient's mental disorder, no matter how mentally or legally incapacitated the patient may be. Sometimes this interface can be somewhat complex. There may be a question as to whether a particular proposed treatment is "for" the patient's mental disorder. For example, is tube-feeding of a patient with anorexia nervosa treatment for the patient's mental illness or treatment for its consequences? The courts have recently decided that a broad view should be taken so that treatment for mental disorder includes treatment for its consequences. This means that some detained patients who have capacity to refuse feeding can nevertheless be treated against their will for physical conditions (ie extreme weight loss) if the physical condition is a consequence of their mental disorder (*B v Croydon District Health Authority*).

1:4 Confidentiality

1:4.1 Lawyers

There is a general principle that "a solicitor is under a duty to keep confidential to his or her firm the affairs of clients and to ensure that the staff do the same": (The Law Society, "The Guide to the Professional Conduct of Solicitors" (6th Edition, 1993)). This general duty is qualified by an exception which states that "express consent by a client to disclosure of information relating to his or her affairs overrides any duty of confidentiality". Although "the duty to keep a client's confidences can be overridden in certain exceptional circumstances", there is no specific exception which permits informing a doctor about the contents of a client's will or the extent of his or her property and affairs, without first having obtained express consent from the client.

However, there have been decisions in cases involving wills in which the judge has stated that there is a "golden if tactless rule" that "when a solicitor is drawing up a will for an aged testator or one who has been seriously ill, it should be witnessed and approved by a medical practitioner, who ought to record his examination of the testator and his findings... (and) that if there was an earlier will it should be examined and any proposed alterations should be discussed with the testator" (*Kenward v*

Adams). Any solicitor who cannot obtain from his or her client the consent to the disclosure of confidential information would be advised to seek the advice of the Professional Ethics Division of the Law Society (address in Appendix C).

1:4.2 Doctors

Doctors are bound by a professional duty to maintain the confidentiality of personal health information unless the patient gives valid consent to disclosure or, if the patient is incapable of giving consent, the doctor believes disclosure to be in that person's best interests. Difficult decisions may arise if relatives, carers or the patient's lawyer approach the doctor for a medical report on an individual whose capacity to understand and consent is in doubt but the patient refuses to be assessed or else agrees to assessment but not to disclosure of the results. Doctors must be guided by what they consider to be the patient's best interests. This includes discussing with patients their needs and preferences. The statutory body for doctors, the General Medical Council, recognises that there are some exceptional circumstances when disclosure of confidential information can be made in the patient's interest without consent (see section 10:7).

1:5 Summary of points for doctors

The following is a brief summary of issues of which doctors should be aware in carrying out an assessment.

- In most situations where a judgment about legal capacity has to be made a doctor's opinion will be obtained. A GP, a consultant, other hospital doctor or a prison or police doctor may be approached to provide this. If the medical practitioner is not routinely involved in assessing capacity, the practical steps outlined in Part IV may provide a helpful guide. Assessment requires a knowledge of the person, including his or her cultural values and social situation. Often more than a brief interview and reading of other medical reports is necessary.

- Capacity, however, is ultimately a legal concept, defined by law. The doctor must assess the person's capacity in relation to whatever activity that person is attempting to carry out. The understanding (legal capacity) required for each decision will depend on the complexity of the information and the legal test (if one exists) to be applied. Doctors who are asked to give an assessment of an individual's capacity must be clear about the relevant legal test (see Part III) and should ask a lawyer to explain it, if necessary.

- A distinction can be drawn between cases where the doctor is assessing an individual's capacity to take an action which is unrelated to receiving medical treatment and assessment of the individual's capacity to consent to medical treatment. In the latter case, doctors have a direct interest in the outcome of the assessment and there will also usually be a presumption that the proposed treatment is in the individual's interests (see section 10:4.3.2 on best interests).

- Every person is entitled to privacy and confidentiality. If the doctor does not know the person, however, it may be necessary to seek views from others with professional and personal knowledge of the individual and knowledge of the specific decision in question. Assessment of whether a person has capacity to manage his or her financial affairs, for example, depends partly on the sums and complexity of the assets involved. A doctor who is asked to provide a medical report in such a case needs some knowledge of the person's assets and the skills required to administer them.

- When asked to assess a person with a learning disability (mental handicap), doctors should not rely on prior reports giving an estimated mental age but ensure that a current assessment is made. Statements of a person's mental age may be misleading if they do not reflect the person's experience and the context for the particular decision. These concerns also apply to people with fluctuating capacity. Assessments of capacity should be regularly reviewed.

- In some circumstances, health professionals may be asked to witness a patient's signature to a legal document. By witnessing the document, it may be inferred that the doctor or nurse is confirming the patient's capacity to enter into the legal transaction effected by the document. Alternatively it may merely indicate that the witness has seen the patient sign the document. Doctors and nurses should be clear as to what they are being asked to do. (See section 2:5 on witnessing documents.)

1:6 Summary of points for lawyers

The following is a brief summary of useful points for lawyers to bear in mind if acting for a person who may lack capacity.

- In carrying out legal transactions or conducting litigation on behalf of their clients, lawyers must act on their client's instructions. They have a duty to advise their clients of the legal consequences of the action they are proposing to take, and clients may change their instructions as a result of receiving legal advice. Ultimately the lawyer must act on the client's instructions, or cease to act on the client's behalf.

- Problems arise where there is doubt as to the client's mental capacity to give instructions. A solicitor cannot accept instructions from a client who does not have mental capacity, except by way of special procedures, for example acting through a receiver, next friend or guardian ad litem (see chapter 6 on capacity to litigate). However, the first step, particularly in borderline cases, is to determine whether or not the client has the capacity to give instructions in relation to the transaction or decision in question.

- There is a legal presumption of capacity unless the contrary is shown. Whether a client has capacity is a matter of law. Different levels of capacity are required for different activities. If there is doubt about a client's mental capacity, it is advisable for the lawyer to seek a medical opinion. Medical practitioners should be asked to give an opinion as to the client's capacity in relation to the particular activity or action in question, rather than a general assessment of the client's mental condition. In order to do this, the lawyer has a responsibility to explain to the doctor the relevant legal test of capacity (see Part III). It should not be assumed that doctors automatically understand what is being asked of them.

- Capacity or lack of it is also a matter of judgment. Doctors' assessments assume more weight in cases which fall into shades of grey rather than those which are clearly black or white. These shades of grey form the majority of cases upon which doctors and lawyers need to liaise. The most obvious cases of incapacity, such as when a person is unconscious or severely mentally impaired, are less likely to require detailed medical confirmation. Similarly, where the person is demonstrably capable of dealing with the matter in hand, medical assessment is superfluous.

- Fluctuating capacity presents difficulties for doctors, which it may be hard to convey to other professionals accustomed to dealing with fact or verifiable certainties. Capacity can be enhanced by the way explanations are given, by the timing of them or by other simple measures discussed in this book. It can be impaired by fatigue, anxiety or unfamiliar surroundings. Yet doctors are constantly working under constraints of time or location and other limitations, including perhaps their own preconceptions or prior reports from other people about the extent of the individual's capacities. Doctors are also trained with the concept of promoting the patient's interests in all circumstances. They may find it difficult to disassociate society's view of what would most benefit the patient from what the patient is actually capable of choosing when that person appears to want something harmful.

1:7 Proposals for law reform

The Law Commission has recently issued a wide-ranging report recommending a major overhaul of the law relating to mental capacity. The focus of the report is decision-making on behalf of those who lack mental capacity to take decisions for themselves. The major recommendation of the Law Commission is that there should be a new statutory jurisdiction within which decisions about a person's personal welfare, medical care and property and affairs can be authorised. The Law Commission has also recommended new powers for local authorities to protect vulnerable adults from abuse and neglect.

The Law Commission's recommendations are currently under review by Government. If the Commission's recommendations are implemented, many of the legal provisions discussed in this book would change. Specific recommendations for reform of the law are mentioned as appropriate throughout this book.

1:7.1 The "best interests" criterion

Both lawyers and doctors need to appreciate that if after an appropriate assessment an individual is judged to lack capacity to make the decision in question, any act or omission taken on that person's behalf must be in that person's best interests. The notion of best interests has been current in the common law for some time (see chapters 10 and 11 on capacity to consent to medical procedures). The Law Commission has recently endorsed the concept of "best interests". The Commission has recommended that in deciding what is in a person's best interests consideration should be given to (a) the past and present wishes of the individual, (b) the need to maximise as much as possible the person's participation in the decision, (c) the views of others as to the person's wishes and feelings and (d) the need to adopt the course of action least restrictive of the individual's freedom. (The Commission's full checklist of best interests factors is included in Appendix A).

1:8 Where to obtain further advice

Both the British Medical Association and the Law Society offer ethical guidance to their members. Doctors can write to the Ethics Department of the BMA and lawyers to the Professional Ethics Division of the Law Society. In addition, advice is also available from bodies such as the Office of the Official Solicitor (see section 6:2) and the Public Trust Office (see section 3:2.1). The addresses of these and other organisations are set out in Appendix C.

PART II

Legal Principles

2 What are the Legal Principles?

2:1 Capacity and the role of the courts

Whether an individual has or lacks capacity to do something is ultimately a question for a court to answer. It is not a decision that can be made conclusively by the family; or the proprietor of a residential care home; or a social worker; or a solicitor; or even a doctor - although their opinions as to capacity may be of assistance in enabling a court to arrive at its own conclusions (*Richmond v Richmond*). Capacity is ultimately a legal question because people with an interest in the outcome may wish to challenge an assessment, either on their own behalf or on behalf of the person who is alleged to lack capacity.

In practice, of course, doctors, solicitors, social workers and others make this sort of decision every hour of the day, every day of the week, and very few cases ever get as far as a court.

Nevertheless, the courts are jealous to safeguard their overall jurisdiction in these matters. By making a decision on capacity, anyone with authority over an individual can deprive that person of civil liberties enjoyed by most adults. Alternatively, such a decision could permit the person lacking capacity to do something, or carry on doing something, whereby serious prejudice could result either to the person lacking capacity or to others. Doctors and lawyers should always bear in mind that, if they decide that someone has or lacks capacity to enter into a transaction, they might have to account to a court for the reasons why they made that decision. It is, therefore, helpful to know what effect an opinion could have on the individual concerned. For example, it could restrict, protect, or empower them. If a case goes to court, the judge has to:

- decide what the facts are; then
- apply the law to those facts; and then
- come to a decision.

Anyone lower down the decision-making chain might find it useful to follow the same steps.

2:2 Capacity and the law of evidence

2:2.1 Presumptions

To keep any investigation of the facts within manageable bounds courts apply various rules of evidence. These are based on conclusions (presumptions) which must, or may, be drawn from particular facts. Presumptions are either irrebuttable or rebuttable. If a presumption is irrebuttable, the court must arrive at a particular conclusion, regardless of any evidence to the contrary. If a presumption is rebuttable, the court has to assume that certain facts are true until the contrary is proved. The most well-known rebuttable presumption is the presumption of innocence: anyone charged with a criminal offence is presumed to be innocent until proved to be guilty. Two important rebuttable presumptions apply to mental capacity; (a) the presumption of competence and (b) the presumption of continuance.

(a) *The presumption of competence*: An individual is presumed to be competent, or to have the mental capacity to enter into a particular transaction, until the contrary is proved.

(b) *The presumption of continuance*: Once it has been proved that someone is incompetent, or lacks capacity, this state of affairs is presumed to continue until the contrary is proved.

2:2.2 Lucid intervals

The presumptions of competence and continuance are rather all or nothing. They tend to suggest that a person is either constantly capable or constantly incapable. Competence can fluctuate, and the name the law gives to an intermittent state of capacity is a "lucid interval". Generally speaking, a deed or document signed by someone who lacks capacity is void and of no effect. But if it is signed during a lucid interval it may be valid.

2:2.3 The burden of proof

Generally, the burden or onus of proof is on the side that has to prove its case. In practical terms this means that if someone alleges something, that person has to prove it. In cases involving mental capacity the burden of proof is affected by the operation of the presumptions of competence and continuance. So, the burden of proof is on the person who alleges that:

- someone lacks capacity (because capacity is presumed until the contrary is proved)
- someone who previously lacked capacity has now recovered and is capable (because incapacity is presumed to continue until the contrary is proved)
- something was validly done by an otherwise incapacitated person during a lucid interval (also because of the presumption of continuance).

The case of *Re Sabatini* illustrates the operation of these rules (this case is discussed in section 4:5). When she was 90 and suffering from Alzheimer's Disease, Mrs Sabatini destroyed a will she had made 25 years earlier leaving everything to her favourite nephew. If she had capacity, her action would have revoked or cancelled the will, and the nephew would have lost his inheritance. Because of the presumption of competence the judge had to presume that Mrs Sabatini had the capacity to revoke the will unless the contrary was proved by acceptable evidence. The burden of proof, therefore, fell on the nephew to prove to the court that his aunt lacked capacity to revoke the will and that the earlier will made in his favour remained in effect. As it turned out, he was able to produce compelling medical evidence of her incapacity at the time she destroyed the will.

2:2.4 The standard of proof

Those on whom the burden of proof rests must prove their case to a particular standard. There are two standards of proof: *beyond reasonable doubt*, which only applies in criminal proceedings; and *the balance of probabilities*, which applies in civil proceedings. In deciding whether or not someone has capacity to enter into a particular transaction or make a particular decision, the standard of proof is the civil standard - the balance of probabilities. In practical terms this is the most important rule of evidence in assessing capacity. Having decided what the facts are, and having applied the law to those facts, the assessor must then decide whether the individual is more likely to have capacity, or more likely to lack capacity to do something.

2:2.5 Character evidence and similar fact evidence

As a general rule, judges will not admit in evidence any information about a person's character or similar events to those now under consideration which have happened in the past. The reason for this rule is that in criminal cases this sort of evidence, although relevant, has a tendency to be prejudicial, and so it is regarded as inadmissible and is not taken into account by the judge. In civil cases, however, a person's psychiatric history is almost always admissible, and is usually highly relevant to the question of capacity.

2:2.6 Opinion evidence and expert evidence

In court proceedings witnesses are usually confined to stating the facts, what they have seen or heard, and are not permitted to express their own opinion. An exception is made in the case of expert witnesses, who are entitled not only to say what they have seen and heard but also to express the opinion they formed as a result. There is no formal definition as to what constitutes expertise. In general, people will be treated as experts if they have devoted time and attention to the particular branch of knowledge involved; if they have had practical experience of it; and, in some cases, if they have acquired a reputation for being skilled in it. Whether or not it is justifiable, the law tends to regard any registered medical practitioner as a de facto expert on mental capacity, and therefore entitled to express an opinion as to whether a person is or was capable of understanding the nature and effects of a particular transaction.

2:2.7 The weight of evidence

Whether or not the burden of proof is discharged depends on the weight and value which the judge attaches to the various strands of evidence. This involves weighing up the credibility or reliability of the evidence, and ultimately comes down to deciding which version of events is more likely to be correct. Although the courts attach a great deal of weight to medical evidence, one doctor's opinion may not be shared by another, and it is not unprecedented for a judge to favour the evidence of someone who is not even medically qualified. For example, in the case of *Birkin v Wing* the judge preferred the evidence of a solicitor, who considered that his client was mentally capable of entering into a particular contract, to that of a doctor who said that the client lacked capacity.

2:3 Practical suggestions for solicitors instructing doctors

If you are a solicitor, and you are asking a doctor to provide medical evidence as to whether or not your client is capable of doing something:

- Don't automatically assume that the doctor is an expert in these matters.
- The quality of the doctor's evidence will depend heavily on the quality of the instructions he or she is given.
- Be clear about the specific capacity that needs to be assessed. For example: capacity to enter into a contract; capacity to marry; capacity to create an enduring power of attorney; capacity to manage and administer one's property and affairs (see Part III).
- Inform the doctor about the legal test to be applied. For example: if the client proposes to make a will, explain to the

doctor the criteria for making a will (see chapter 4).

- Explain the legal test in simple language that an ordinary, intelligent person, who is not a qualified lawyer, can understand. For example: say what is meant by the nature and effect of a particular document.

- Let the doctor have all the relevant information needed to enable him or her to express an informed opinion. For example: if an application is being made to the Court of Protection for the appointment of a receiver, the doctor will need to know something about the client's property and affairs in order to assess whether or not that client is "incapable, by reason of mental disorder, of managing and administering" such property and affairs (but see section 1:4 on confidentiality).

- Make sure that the doctor is aware that the standard of proof is *the balance of probabilities*, rather than *beyond reasonable doubt*.

- It may be worth reminding the doctor that his or her opinion on the client's capacity is open to challenge (and as a courtesy the doctor should be informed if the matter is likely to be contentious, without giving the impression that a lower standard of care will suffice in a non-contentious case).

- If possible, try to avoid asking for simultaneous assessments of the client's capacity for a variety of different transactions. For example: where a client is in the early stages of dementia, it would be unreasonable to expect the doctor to assess in one examination whether the client is capable of making a will, creating an enduring power of attorney, making a lifetime gift, and managing and administering his or her property and affairs. Not only is it unfair to the doctor, it could also be extremely unfair to the client.

2:4 Practical suggestions for doctors receiving instructions from solicitors

If you are a doctor, and a solicitor asks you to assess someone's capacity:

- Don't be afraid to decline the instructions if you feel that you have insufficient knowledge or practical experience to make a proper assessment of capacity. Having said that, a GP who sees his or her patient on a fairly regular basis is likely to be in a better position to say what the patient is capable or incapable of doing than a specialist who has seen the patient only once or twice.

- Don't automatically assume that the solicitor is an expert in these matters or that he or she has told you everything you need to know.

- Don't be afraid to ask for further information about: (a) details of the test of capacity that the law requires with an explanation of that test in simple language that an ordinary intelligent person who is not legally qualified can understand; (b) why your opinion is being sought, and what effect your opinion might have on the patient or client; (c) about the patient's property, affairs and family background if you think they are relevant to the particular type of capacity to be assessed; and (d) whether the matter is likely to be contentious or disputed, but don't be pressurised into making a decision that will please the solicitor or the patient's family or one faction of the patient's family.

- Wherever possible, keep your report specific, rather than general, in its terms. Remember that: a laconic opinion lacking detail, diagnosis and reasons is likely to be of little value in terms of evidence; your opinion could deprive the individual of a liberty that most adults enjoy; your opinion could allow the individual to do something, or to carry on doing something, which could be extremely prejudicial to the individual or somebody else; your opinion could affect the availability of certain financial benefits or services; and that you might have to give an account in court of the reasons why you arrived at a particular opinion.

2:5 Witnessing documents

Medical professionals, especially those working in hospitals, are often reluctant to witness a patient's signature on a document. Indeed, many health authorities and trusts specifically prohibit their personnel from acting as witnesses. This is understandable because, more often than not, the professional status of a doctor or nurse is being invoked in order to lend greater credibility to a transaction. In the section on capacity and the law of evidence (see section 2:2.6) a distinction was drawn between ordinary witnesses and expert witnesses. Ordinary witnesses are expected merely to state what they have seen or heard. So, when it comes to witnessing a signature on a document, an ordinary witness simply states that the document was signed by a person in his or her presence. Expert witnesses are in a different position, because they are invited not only to say what they have seen or heard but also to express an opinion. As was mentioned earlier, the law regards medical practitioners as de facto experts on mental capacity. So when a doctor witnesses someone's signature on a document there is a strong inference that the patient had the requisite capacity to enter into the transaction effected by the document.

In some cases, however, the law virtually demands that a doctor should witness a patient's signature. For example, in *Kenward v Adams* the judge laid down what he called "the golden rule" that, where a will has been drawn up for an elderly person or for someone who is seriously ill, it should be witnessed or approved by a medical practitioner. The judge assumed that the doctor would not only make a formal assessment of capacity but also record his or her examination and findings. It is recommended therefore that, in cases where there is any doubt about a patient's capacity to enter into a particular transaction, doctors and nurses should not witness the patient's signature on a document unless:

- they have formally assessed the patient's capacity; and
- they are satisfied that, on the balance of probabilities, the patient has the requisite capacity to enter into the transaction effected by a document; and
- they make a formal record of their examination and findings.

We reproduce here a sample form for a Certificate of Capacity which may be useful to doctors who are called upon to witness documents.

2:5.1 Sample Certificate of Capacity

1. **I** *(full name and professional qualifications of medical practitioner)* **of** *(address)* **CERTIFY as follows**

2. *(full name and date of birth of patient)* **has been a patient of mine since** *(date)* **and I have seen [him] [her]** *(describe in general terms the degree of regularity; eg. approximately four times a year)*

3. **On** *(date)* **I examined the patient for the purpose of assessing whether [he][she] is capable of** *(describe the transaction: eg., making a will; signing an enduring power of attorney)*

4. **In my opinion the patient is [not suffering from any mental disability] [OR, suffering from mental disability namely** *(describe the mental disability: eg. dementia)*]

5. **In my opinion the patient is [capable][incapable] of** *(describe the transaction, as in paragraph 3 above)*

6. **I base my opinion on the following grounds:** *(state the reasons)*

Signed ....

Dated ....

PART III

Legal Tests of Capacity

3 Capacity to Deal With Financial Affairs

3:1 Powers of attorney

A power of attorney is a deed by which one person (*the donor*) gives another person (*the attorney*) the authority to act in the donor's name and on his or her behalf in relation to the donor's property and financial affairs. A power of attorney can be *specific* or *general*. If it is specific, the attorney only has the authority to do the things specified by the donor in the power. If it is general, the attorney has the authority to do "anything that the donor can lawfully do by an attorney". The law imposes certain restrictions on what actions a donor can delegate to an attorney. For example, an attorney cannot execute a will on the donor's behalf, nor act in situations which require the personal knowledge of the donor (such as acting as a witness in court). Therefore under a general power of attorney, the attorney only has the authority to do what the donor can lawfully delegate to someone else.

There are two types of powers of attorney:

(a) an *ordinary power of attorney* which ceases to have effect if the donor becomes mentally incapable; and

(b) an *enduring power of attorney* which "endures" or continues to operate after the donor has become mentally incapable, provided that it is registered with the Court of Protection (see section 3:2.1).

3:1.1 Ordinary powers of attorney

The test of capacity which a person must satisfy in order to make a power of attorney is that the donor understands the nature and effect of what he or she is doing. An ordinary power of attorney (one which is not "enduring") tends to be used as a temporary expedient: for example, where the donor is going abroad for several months and needs someone to look after various legal or financial transactions during his or her absence. The traditional view is that the capacity required to create an ordinary power of attorney is co-existent with the donor's capacity to do the act which the attorney is authorised to do. If there is any doubt as to the donor's capacity to do the act in question, it would be advisable for the donor to create an enduring power, rather than an ordinary power, so long as he or she has the requisite capacity to do so (see section 3:1.3).

3:1.2 Enduring powers of attorney (EPAs)

Enduring powers became available in England and Wales in March 1986, when the Enduring Powers of Attorney Act 1985 came into force. Over 15,000 EPAs have been registered with the Court of Protection. The Act itself says nothing about the degree of understanding the donor needs in order to make a valid enduring power - this point was later settled in a court case - but it does require the power to be in the form prescribed by the Lord Chancellor. The prescribed form contains most of the basic relevant information that the donor needs to understand, and the procedures to be adopted when *executing*, or signing, an enduring power.

The prescribed form is divided into three parts.

- Part A is a page of information explaining what an enduring power is; how the prescribed form should be completed;

when and how the power should be registered with the Court of Protection; and informing the donor that they can cancel the power at any time before it has to be registered. It is essential to the validity of an enduring power that the explanatory notes in Part A are read by or to the donor before he or she signs Part B of the prescribed form.

- Part B contains the actual appointment of the attorney(s), and it should be executed, or signed, by the donor in the presence of one witness. A second witness is only necessary if the form is not signed by the donor personally but by someone else in the donor's presence and at his or her direction (possibly because a physical disability prevents the donor from signing it personally).

- Part C explains some of the duties of an attorney and should be executed by the attorney in the presence of a witness.

Unless the enduring power specifically states that it will not come into force until the donor is mentally incapacitated (which is rare), the power is "live" from the moment the donor executes it. In other words, the attorney can act under it straightaway, even though the donor may still be perfectly capable of looking after his or her own property and affairs. If the enduring power is not registered with the Court of Protection, the donor and the attorney have what is known as *concurrent authority*. Both of them can manage and administer the donor's property and affairs.

An attorney acting under an enduring power must apply to the Court of Protection for the registration of the power if the attorney has reason to believe that the donor is, or is becoming, incapable, by reason of mental disorder, of managing and administering his or her property and affairs.

The donor and his or her nearest relatives must be informed of the attorney's intention to register the power. There is a statutory list of relatives in a Schedule to the Enduring Powers of Attorney Act 1985 which is similar to, but not the same as, the list of nearest relatives in the Mental Health Act 1983. Both the donor and the relatives have the right to object to the registration of the power: for example, if relatives believe that the donor is not yet incapable of managing his or her affairs, or that the power may be invalid. Once the power has been registered by the Court of

Protection, the donor and the attorney no longer have concurrent authority. Only the attorney has the authority to manage and administer the donor's property and affairs. However, if even after registration the donor has capacity to perform small tasks such as running a bank account or shopping, the fact that the power has been registered should not as matter of practice, prevent others from relying on the donor's instructions.

3:1.3 Capacity to make an EPA

It was, and still is, the law that a power of attorney signed by a person who lacks capacity is null and void, unless it can be proved that it was signed during a lucid interval. Shortly after the Enduring Powers of Attorney Act 1985 came into force the Court of Protection received a considerable number of applications to register enduring powers which had only just been created. This raised a doubt as to whether the donors had been mentally capable when they signed the powers. The problem was resolved in the test cases *Re K, Re F,* in which the judge discussed the capacity to create an enduring power.

Having stated that the test of capacity to create an enduring power of attorney was that the donor understood the nature and effect of the document, the judge in the case set out four pieces of information which any person creating an EPA should understand:

- firstly, if such be the terms of the power, that the attorney will be able to assume complete authority over the donor's affairs;
- secondly, if such be the terms of the power, that the attorney will be able to do anything with the donor's property which the donor could have done;
- thirdly, that the authority will continue if the donor should be or should become mentally incapable; and
- fourthly, that if he or she should be or should become mentally incapable, the power will be irrevocable without confirmation by the Court of Protection.

It is worth noting that the donor need not have the capacity to do all the things which the attorney will be able to do under the power. The donor need only have capacity to create the EPA.

3:1.4 The implications of Re K, Re F

The judge in *Re K, Re F* also commented that if the donor is capable of signing an enduring power of attorney, but incapable of managing and administering his or her property and affairs, the attorney has an obligation to register the power with the Court of Protection straightaway. In fact, nearly half of the applications for registration received by the Court of Protection involve enduring powers which have been created less than three months before the application was made. Arguably, the attorney also has a moral duty in such cases to forewarn the donor that registration is not merely possible, but is intended immediately.

The decision in *Re K, Re F* has been criticised for imposing too simple a test of capacity to create an enduring power. But the simplicity or complexity of the test depends largely on the questions asked by the person assessing the donor's capacity. For example, if the four pieces of basic relevant information described by the judge in *Re K, Re F* were mentioned to the donor and he or she was asked "Do you understand this?" in such a way as to encourage an affirmative reply, the donor would probably pass the test with flying colours and, indeed, the test would be too simple. If, on the other hand, the assessor were specifically to ask the donor "What will your attorney be able to do?" and "What will happen if you become mentally incapable?" the test would be substantially harder. There is no direct judicial authority on the point, but it can be inferred from the decision in *Re Beaney (deceased)*, that questions susceptible to the answers "Yes" or "No" may be inadequate for the purpose of assessing capacity.

Although the legislation does not require the donor's execution of an enduring power of attorney to be witnessed by a doctor, where the donor is of borderline capacity it is advisable that the power be witnessed or approved by a medical practitioner who should record his or her findings: see *Kenward v Adams* which is discussed in sections 2:5 and 4:3.

3:1.5 Capacity to revoke a power of attorney

Until an application for registration has been made, the donor may revoke or destroy a power of attorney at any time. If the donor does so, but the attorney believes the donor lacks the capacity to revoke the power, the attorney can apply for registration of the power. The donor may then object to the registration on the ground that the power is no longer valid, and the Court must decide whether this ground for objection is established.

After registration, no revocation of an enduring power by the donor is valid unless and until the Court of Protection confirms the revocation. In either situation, the Court applies the principle that donors must have the same degree of capacity when revoking or destroying an enduring power as they had when they made it. This is consistent with the principle in *Re Sabatini*, that the same degree of capacity is required to revoke a will as to make one (see section 4:5).

It is understood that, in practice, where the donor of a registered enduring power wishes to revoke it, the attorney often disclaims, that is, gives notice to the Court that he or she wishes to cease acting as attorney. The Court must then decide whether the donor has capacity to resume management of his or her own affairs, or whether a receivership order or some other order should be made in respect of the donor (see section 3:2).

3:1.6 Proposals for law reform

In its recent report the Law Commission has recommended the repeal of the Enduring Powers of Attorney Act 1985. In its place the Commission recommends the creation of a new type of power of attorney called a Continuing Power of Attorney. Like an EPA this new power would endure even after the donor has lost capacity. However, unlike the existing scheme, the Commission recommends that it should be possible to appoint an attorney to take decisions about the donor's personal welfare and medical treatment as well as the person's property and financial affairs.

3:2 Capacity to manage property and affairs

If a person who has not made an enduring power of attorney becomes incapable, by reason of mental disorder, of managing and administering his or her property and affairs, it may be necessary for someone to apply to the Court of Protection for the appointment of a *receiver* to deal with the day-to-day management of that person's affairs.

The Court of Protection is required to look at medical evidence before it considers appointing a receiver. The Court's rules specifically state that the evidence must be provided by a registered medical practitioner who is expected to complete a printed Medical Certificate known as Form CP3. In consultation with the Royal College of Psychiatrists and the British Medical Association the Court has prepared a set of notes which accompany Form CP3 and which provide useful guidelines as to the sort of information the Court is looking for. Ideally, any doctor who completes a Form CP3 should know something about:

- the Court of Protection;
- mental disorder;
- the patient;
- the patient's property and affairs; and
- how to assess whether a person is incapable, by reason of mental disorder, of managing and administering their property and affairs.

3:2.1 The Court of Protection

The Court of Protection is described in Part VII of the Mental Health Act 1983. It is an office of the Supreme Court, and its function is to oversee the management of the property and affairs of people who are mentally disordered, as defined below. Its origins go back to the Middle Ages when the Crown assumed the responsibility of managing the estates of the mentally ill and mentally handicapped. The head of the Court of Protection is called the Master. People whose affairs are managed by the Court are known as "patients". Since 1987 the Court has shared premises with the Public Trust Office (PTO). The PTO is responsible for the overall running of the patient's financial affairs in conjunction with the receiver, and for the paperwork involved in the registration of enduring powers of attorney. The head of the PTO is known as the Public Trustee. The Public Trust Office looks after the affairs of more than 30,000 patients. Its average annual intake of new receivership cases is about 7,000, and the average number of enduring powers it registers each year is roughly the same.

The Court of Protection itself deals with the appointment of receivers and decides any contentious issues and the more serious questions arising in a receivership. If it requires a specialist opinion about a person's mental capacity, the Court may instruct one of the Lord Chancellor's Visitors to visit the patient and produce a report. There are six *Medical Visitors*. Each is a senior consultant psychiatrist, and each is responsible for a particular area of England and Wales. The main function of a receiver appointed by the Court of Protection is to receive and deal with the patient's income. However, if the order appointing the receiver so permits, he or she has the authority to do anything necessary to ensure the proper management of the patient's property and affairs.

Anyone who is aggrieved by a decision or order of the Court of Protection may appeal to a nominated High Court Judge (all judges of the Chancery Division have been nominated). Appeals from the Judge are heard by the Court of Appeal, and appeals from the Court of Appeal are heard by the House of Lords.

3:2.2 Mental disorder

For a person to come within the jurisdiction of the Court of Protection it is necessary to prove two things: firstly, that the person is suffering from mental disorder; **and** secondly that, because of the mental disorder, the person is incapable of managing and administering his or her property and affairs. These two conditions do not automatically coincide. People suffering from mental disorder might be quite capable of looking after their financial affairs and those who are not mentally disordered may be completely hopeless in running their affairs; they could be disorganised, uninterested, foolish, prodigal, or just lazy.

Mental disorder is defined in section 1(2) of the Mental Health Act 1983 as:

> mental illness, arrested or incomplete development of mind [more commonly referred to as mental handicap or learning disability], psychopathic disorder [a persistent disorder or disability of mind which results in abnormally aggressive or seriously irresponsible conduct] and any other disorder or disability of mind [which covers disorders arising from, say, a brain injury].

Section 1(3) of the Act states that people must not be regarded as suffering from mental disorder by reason only of (a) promiscuity or other immoral conduct, (b) sexual deviancy or dependence on alcohol or drugs.

Mental illness is not actually defined in the Mental Health Act 1983. A senior judge has suggested that these words "have no particular medical significance; no particular legal significance; and that they should be interpreted in the way that any ordinary, sensible person would interpret them" (*W v L*).

In an appendix to "A Review of the Mental Health Act 1959" published in 1976, the Department of Health and Social Security suggested the following guidelines on the clinical symptoms commonly associated with mental illness:

> "*Mental illness* means an illness having one or more of the following characteristics:
>
> (i) More than temporary impairment of intellectual functions shown by a failure of memory, orientation, comprehension, and learning capacity; (ii) More than temporary alteration of mood of such a degree as to give rise to the patient having a delusional appraisal of his situation, his past or his future, or that of others, or to the lack of any appraisal; (iii) Delusional beliefs, persecutory, jealous or grandiose; (iv) Abnormal perceptions associated with delusional interpretation of events; (v) Thinking so disordered as to prevent the patient making a reasonable appraisal of his situation or having reasonable communication with others." (quoted in *Jones* "Mental Health Act Manual" 1994).

This definition has been criticised by some psychiatrists because it is restrictive in some places and over-inclusive in others, and because it seems to exclude the commonest psychiatric disorder encountered in practice which is depression.

3:2.3 Property and affairs

Assessing a patient's capacity to manage and administer his or her property and affairs is extremely subjective to the patient. The patient's ability to cope depends largely on the value and complexity of the property and affairs, and the extent to which the patient may be vulnerable to exploitation. It has been held that "property and affairs" means business matters, legal transactions, and other dealings of a similar kind (*Re F (Mental Patient: Sterilisation)*). It does not include matters such as where to live or medical treatment decisions.

3:2.4 Checklist

The following checklist is not intended to be exhaustive or authoritative, but simply to give some indication of the wide range of information which may be needed in order to make a proper assessment of a person's capacity to manage his or her property and affairs. It is worth emphasising again that the presence of a mental disorder is a pre-requisite to a conclusion that a person lacks capacity to manage and administer his or her property and affairs.

3:2.4.1 The extent of the person's property and affairs

This would include an examination of:

- the value of a person's income and capital (including savings and the value of the home);
- financial needs and responsibilities;
- whether there are likely to be any changes in the person's financial circumstances in the foreseeable future;
- the skill, specialised knowledge and time it takes to manage the affairs properly and whether the mental disorder is affecting the management of the assets;
- whether the person would be likely to seek, understand and act on appropriate advice where needed in view of the complexity of the affairs.

3:2.4.2 Personal information

Personal information about the patient might include: age; life expectancy; psychiatric history; prospects of recovery or deterioration; the extent to which the incapacity could fluctuate; the condition in which the person lives; family background; family and social responsibilities; the degree of back-up and support the person receives or could expect to receive from others.

3:2.4.3 A person's vulnerability

Other issues which should be considered might be:

- Could inability to manage the property and affairs lead to the person making rash or irresponsible decisions?
- Could inability to manage lead to exploitation by others - perhaps even members of the person's family?

- Could inability to manage lead to the position of other people being compromised or jeopardised?

3:2.5 Proposals for law reform

If implemented, recommendations made by the Law Commission would significantly alter the jurisdiction of the Court of Protection. The new Court of Protection recommended by the Commission would have powers to make decisions about the personal welfare, medical treatment and property and affairs of a person without capacity.

3:3 Capacity to claim and receive social security benefits

There is a statutory mechanism through which social security benefits may be claimed on behalf of a person lacking capacity.

3:3.1 Appointeeship

If the claimant is *mentally* incapable of managing his or her affairs, the Secretary of State can appoint an individual aged 18 or over (known as an *appointee*) to:

(a) exercise any rights and duties the claimant has under the Social Security Acts and Regulations. For example: claiming benefits; establishing "good cause" for any delay in making a claim; informing the Department of any change in the claimant's circumstances; and appealing against the decision of an adjudication officer; and

(b) receive any benefits payable to the claimant; and

(c) deal with the money received on the claimant's behalf in the interests of the claimant and his or her dependents.

Appointeeship is governed by Regulation 33 of the Social Security (Claims and Payments) Regulations 1987 which says that an appointee may be appointed by the Secretary of State where:

> "a person is, or is alleged to be, entitled to benefit, whether or not a claim for benefit has been made by him or on his behalf; and
>
> that person is unable for the time being to act; and
>
> no receiver has been appointed by the Court of Protection

with power to claim or, as the case may be, receive benefit on his behalf."

The test of capacity is therefore that the person is "for the time being unable to act". The Regulation does not define this phrase, but the Department of Social Security's internal guidance suggests that people may be unable to act if "they do not have the mental ability to understand and control their own affairs, for example, because of senility or mental illness".

The application for the appointment of an appointee (Form BF56), which is usually completed by the person applying to be appointed, states that "You may be asked to produce medical evidence of the claimant's inability to manage his own affairs". The Department does not require medical evidence in all cases, and does not provide any standard form of medical certificate.

The Secretary of State can revoke an appointment at any time, and there is no right of appeal to a tribunal against the Secretary of State's refusal to appoint a particular individual as appointee or against the revocation of such an appointment. Appointees have no authority to deal with the claimant's capital. If the claimant has capital and it needs to be applied or invested, an application should be made to the Public Trust Office for directions as to how to proceed. The Law Commission has recently made suggestions for reform of the appointee scheme.

4 Capacity to Make a Will

4:1 Introduction

A will is a document in which the maker (called the *testator*) if he is a man, and the *testatrix* if she is a woman) appoints an executor to deal with his or her affairs when the person dies, and describes how the person's estate is to be distributed after death. Subject to a few exceptions the maker of a will must be aged 18 or over. A will comes into operation only on the maker's death. Until then the person can revoke the will or make a new one at any time, provided that he or she still has the capacity to do so. The making of a new will revokes any previous will provided the person making the will had the capacity to do so (see section 4:5 on capacity to revoke a will).

Someone who dies without leaving a valid will is said to die intestate. The person responsible for sorting out an intestate's affairs is called an administrator, and that person has a duty to distribute the estate to the intestate's relatives in the shares set out in the Administration of Estates Act 1925 (as amended).

About 10% of the wills made in England and Wales are home-made - handwritten or typed by the person making it - usually on a pre-printed form bought at a stationer's or Post Office. In most cases, however, people ask a solicitor to prepare a will for them. The solicitor advises them of the various options; prepares a draft will based on these discussions; and sends a copy of the draft to the client for approval. The draft is then approved or amended, and the will is engrossed, or fair-copied, in readiness for executing, or signing.

The degree of understanding which the law requires a person making a will to have is commonly known as *testamentary capacity*. People making a will should have testamentary capacity both (a) when they give instructions to a solicitor for the preparation of the will (or, in the case of a home-made will, when they write or type it), and (b) when they execute, or sign, the will.

4:2 Testamentary capacity

The most important case on testamentary capacity is *Banks v Goodfellow*. In this case the testator, John Banks, was a bachelor in his fifties who lived with his teenaged niece, Margaret Goodfellow. He was a paranoid schizophrenic and was convinced that a grocer (who was, in fact, dead) was pursuing and persecuting him. In 1863, with his solicitor's assistance, he made a short and simple will leaving his entire estate (fifteen houses) to Margaret. He died in 1865 and Margaret inherited the estate.

Nobody would have questioned the validity of this will were it not for the fact that Margaret died shortly after coming into her inheritance. She was under age and unmarried, and the fifteen properties passed to her half-brother, who was not related to John Banks. The will was contested by various members of the Banks family on the grounds that, when he made the will, John had lacked testamentary capacity because of his paranoid delusions. The court held that partial unsoundness of mind, which has no influence on the way in which a testator disposes of his property, is not sufficient to make a person incapable of validly disposing of his property by will. So John Banks's will was valid.

The Lord Chief Justice set out the following criteria for testamentary capacity:

> "It is essential ... that a testator shall understand the nature of the act and its effects; shall understand the extent of the property of which he is disposing; shall be able to comprehend and appreciate the claims to which he ought to give effect; and, with a view to the latter object, that no disorder of mind shall poison his affections, pervert his sense of right, or prevent the exercise of his natural faculties - that no insane delusion shall influence his will in disposing of his property and bring about a disposal of it which, if the mind had been sound, would not have been made."

The first elements (understanding the nature of the act and its effects, and the extent of the property being disposed of) involve the will-maker's understanding: in other words, the ability to receive and evaluate information which may possibly be communicated by others. The final test (being able to comprehend the claims to which he or she ought to give effect) goes beyond understanding and requires the person making the will to be able to distinguish and compare potential beneficiaries and arrive at some form of judgment. A person making a will can, if mentally capable, ignore the claims of relatives and other potential beneficiaries.

Everyone has the right to be capricious, foolish, biased or prejudiced, and it is important to remember that, when some-one's capacity is being assessed, it is the ability to make a decision (not necessarily a sensible or wise decision) that is under scrutiny. In the case of *Bird v Luckie* the judge specifically remarked that, although the law requires a person to be capable of understanding the nature and effect of an action, it does not insist that the person behave "in such a manner as to deserve approbation from the prudent, the wise, or the good". People without capacity should be given the same latitude as everyone else, especially where their capriciousness, foolishness, bias or prejudice existed before the onset of mental disability.

It is not clear how far a solicitor or doctor, say, can assist in enhancing the capacity of someone who is making a will. An explanation in broad terms and simple language of relevant basic information about the nature and effect of the will is probably in order. Within reason, the person making the will could also be reminded of the extent of his or her assets. But the final test, being able to comprehend and appreciate the claims to which he or she ought to give effect, is one that the testator or testatrix must pass unaided. There is a substantial body of judicial authority which insists that "unquestionably, there must be a complete and absolute proof that the party who had so formed the will did it without any assistance" (*Cartwright v Cartwright*) and that "a disposing mind and memory is one able to comprehend, of its own initiative and volition, the essential elements of will-making... merely to be able to make rational responses is not enough, nor to repeat a tutored formula of simple terms" (*Leger v Poirier*).

4:3 Supervening incapacity

Occasionally a person becomes ill, or his or her condition deteriorates, between giving instructions for the preparation of a will and executing it. In these circumstances, if the will has been prepared strictly in accordance with the instructions given, it may still be valid even though, when it is executed, the person merely recalls giving instructions to the solicitor and believes that the will being executed complies with those instructions. This is known as the rule in *Parker v Felgate*. This case concerned a 28 year old widow, Mrs Compton, who suffered from glomerulonephritis, or Bright's Disease. In July 1882 she consulted her solicitor about making a new will. She wanted to leave £500 to her father, £250 to her brother, and the rest of her estate (about £2,500) to Great Ormond Street Hospital. During August she experienced extreme renal failure. The will was drawn up on the basis of the earlier instructions, and it was signed by someone else in her presence and at her direction, as the law permits. Four days later the testatrix died. Her father and brother, who would have benefitted on her intestacy, contested the will on the grounds that she lacked testamentary capacity when the will was executed.

The judge held that in a case of this nature three questions must be asked:

(1) when the will was executed, did she remember and understand the instructions she had given to her solicitor?

(2) if it had been thought advisable to stimulate her, could she have understood each clause of the will when it was explained to her? and

(3) was she capable of understanding, and did she understand, that she was executing a will for which she had previously given instructions to her solicitor?

These questions should be asked in the order of priority listed above, and if the answer to any one of them is "Yes", the will shall be valid. On the evidence in this particular case the jury answered "No" to the first two questions, and "Yes" to the third, and accordingly Mrs Compton's will was valid and Great Ormond Street Hospital got its legacy.

The same principle applies when the person making a will has written or typed it and that person's condition deteriorates between preparing the will and executing it (*In the Estate of Wallace: Solicitor of the Duchy of Cornwall v Batten*).

There is a "golden rule" that a solicitor, when drawing up a will for an elderly person or someone who is seriously ill, should ensure that the will is witnessed or approved by a medical practitioner. The medical practitioner should record his or her examination and findings and, where there is an earlier will, it should be examined and any proposed alterations should be discussed with the testator or testatrix (*Kenward v Adams*).

4:4 Checklist

The following checklist gives some idea of what is meant by "understanding the nature of the act and its effects", "understanding the extent of the property being disposed of", and being "able to comprehend and appreciate the claims to which a person making a will ought to give effect". The checklist is not intended to be either authoritative or exhaustive.

4:4.1 The nature of the act

People making a will should understand that:

- they will die;
- the will shall come into operation on their death, but not before; and
- they can change or revoke the will at any time before their death, provided they have the capacity to do so.

4:4.2 The effects of making a will

People making a will should also understand:

- who the executor is or who the executors are (and perhaps why they should be appointed as executors);
- who gets what under the will;
- whether a beneficiary's gift is outright or conditional (for example, where the beneficiary is only entitled to the income from a lump sum during his or her lifetime, or is allowed to occupy residential property for the rest of the beneficiary's life);
- that if they spend their money or give away or sell their property during their lifetime, the beneficiaries might lose out;
- that a beneficiary might die before them; and
- whether they have already made a will and, if so, how and why the new will differs from the old one.

4:4.3 The extent of the property

It is important to note that the judge in *Banks v Goodfellow* used the word extent, rather than value. Practical difficulties can arise when the investments of the person making the will are managed by somebody else and there are no recent statements or valuations. In these cases a reasonableness test should be applied to any estimate the person making the gift gives about the extent of his or her wealth. People making a will should understand:

- the extent of all the property owned solely by them;
- the fact that certain types of jointly-owned property might automatically pass to the other joint owner, regardless of anything that is said in the will;
- whether there are benefits payable on their death which might be unaffected by the terms of their will (insurance policies, pension rights etc); and
- that the extent of their property could change during their lifetime.

4:4.4 The claims of others

People making a will should also be able to comprehend and appreciate the claims to which they ought to give effect, and their reasons for preferring some beneficiaries and, perhaps excluding others. For example possible beneficiaries:

- may already have received adequate provision from the person;
- may be financially better-off than others;
- may have been more attentive or caring than others; or
- may be in greater need of assistance because of their age, gender, or physical or mental problems.

4:5 Capacity to revoke a will

When a will is revoked it is cancelled, and will no longer come into effect on its maker's death. A will can be revoked in three ways:

(a) if the person who made it subsequently gets married, the will is automatically revoked by operation of law, unless it was specifically made in expectation of that marriage (see section 9:2

on capacity to consent to marriage). If a person who lacks testamentary capacity marries (thereby revoking a previous will) it may be necessary to apply to the Court of Protection for the making of a statutory will (see section 4:6);

(b) by making another will or signing a document which expressly states that the earlier will is revoked. In this case the usual rules on testamentary capacity apply; or

(c) if, with the intention of revoking it, the maker personally burns, tears or destroys the will, or authorises somebody else to burn, tear or destroy it in the maker's presence.

The capacity required to revoke a will by destroying it was considered in the case of *Re Sabatini*. In June 1940 Mrs Ruth Sabatini executed a will in which she left a few legacies to various friends and relatives and the rest of her estate to her favourite nephew, Anthony. On 16 September 1965 she tore up this will. On 24 November 1965 she was diagnosed as suffering from senile dementia. She died in May 1966, aged 91. If the will had been validly revoked, Mrs Sabatini would have died intestate, and the whole of her estate (worth just over £50,000) would have been distributable among eight nephews and nieces; each getting an equal share. Anthony sought probate of a carbon copy of the 1940 will, and realised that the burden was on him to prove that his aunt was not of sound mind, memory and understanding when she tore up her will. He produced compelling medical evidence to support his case.

The barrister representing the other seven nephews and nieces put forward the argument that a lower standard of capacity, a lesser degree of concentration, was acceptable when a will is destroyed, and that a person who was incapable of making a new will might understand that a beneficiary had become unworthy of his or her inheritance and wish to deprive the beneficiary of it by tearing up the will and dying intestate. The judge rejected this argument, and said that as a general rule an individual must have the same standard of mind and memory and the same degree of understanding when destroying a will as when making one. Taking all the evidence in this case, and regarding the events of 16 September in the light of what had happened before and Mrs Sabatini's condition afterwards, the only possible conclusion was that the destruction of her will was not "a rational act rationally done". She did not have the capacity to revoke her will, and the carbon copy of the 1940 will was admitted to probate.

Re Sabatini establishes that a person who intends to revoke his or her will must be capable of:

- understanding the nature of the act of revoking a will;
- understanding the effect of revoking the will (this might even involve a greater understanding of the operation of the intestacy rules than is necessary for the purpose of making a will, although there is no direct authority on the point and it would be extremely difficult to prove retrospectively);
- understanding the extent of his or her property; and
- comprehending and appreciating the claims to which he or she ought to give effect.

4:6 Statutory wills

If a person is both (a) incapable, by reason of mental disorder, of managing and administering his or her property and affairs, and (b) incapable of making a valid will for himself or herself, an application can be made to the Court of Protection for what is known as a statutory will to be drawn up and executed on the person's behalf. The Court requires medical evidence of both types of incapacity (see section 3:2). The fact that a person is a patient of the Court of Protection does not mean that the person lacks testamentary capacity. If the person has testamentary capacity a solicitor can be instructed and the will drawn up under the direction of the Court of Protection.

When deciding what provisions should be included in a statutory will the Court of Protection has regard to the following five principles which were laid down in the case of *Re D(J)*:

(1) it is to be assumed that the patient is having a brief lucid interval at the time when the will is made;

(2) it is to be assumed that during the lucid interval the patient has a full knowledge of the past and a full realisation that, as soon as the will is executed, he or she will relapse into the actual mental

state that previously existed, with the prognosis as it actually is;

(3) it is the actual patient who has to be considered and not a hypothetical patient;

(4) during the hypothetical lucid interval the patient is to be envisaged as being advised by competent solicitors; and

(5) in all normal cases the patient is to be envisaged as taking a broad brush to the claims on his or her bounty, rather than an accountant's pen.

5 Capacity to Make a Gift

5:1 Introduction

It is not uncommon for people, especially older people, to give away some or most of their assets to others-usually their children or grandchildren. Often a gift is made to reduce the amount of tax payable on their death, and the law regards tax avoidance - as distinct from tax evasion - as an entirely legitimate exercise. Sometimes a gift is made for other reasons: perhaps to prevent assets falling into the hands of creditors on bankruptcy; or to enable the giver to claim Social Security benefits or be funded by local Social Services if the person has to go into a residential care home or nursing home. Parliament has anticipated most of these schemes and the relevant legislation usually contains lengthy anti-avoidance provisions which could render such disposals ineffective.

Anyone who is asked to assess whether a person is capable of making a gift should (a) not let the underlying purpose or motive affect the assessment, unless it is so perverse as to cast doubt on capacity and (b) be satisfied that the giver is acting freely and voluntarily, and that nobody is pressurising the person into making a gift.

5:2 The test of capacity

The most important case on capacity to make a gift is *Re Beaney (Deceased)*. In that case a 64 year old widow with three grown up children owned and lived in a three-bedroom semi-detached house. Her elder daughter lived with her. In May 1973, a few days after being admitted to hospital suffering from advanced dementia, the widow signed a deed of gift transferring the house to her elder daughter. The widow died intestate the following year, and her son and younger daughter applied successfully to the court for a declaration that the transfer of the house was void and of no effect because their mother was mentally incapable of making such a gift. The judge in the case set out the following criteria for capacity to make a lifetime gift:

"The degree or extent of understanding required in respect of any instrument is relative to the particular transaction which it is to effect. ...Thus, at one extreme, if the subject-matter and value of a gift are trivial in relation to the donor's other assets, a low degree of understanding will suffice. But, at the other, if its effect is to dispose of the donor's only asset of value and thus, for practical purposes, to pre-empt the devolution of his estate under [the donor's] will or ...intestacy, then the degree of understanding required is as high as that required for a will, and the donor must understand the claims of all potential donees and the extent of the property to be disposed of."

It is arguable that, when someone makes a substantial gift, a further point should be considered, namely, the effect that disposing of the asset could have on the donor for the rest of his or her life.

5:3 Checklist

This checklist looks at some of the points that may need to be considered in order to establish whether someone has the capacity to make a lifetime gift of a substantial asset. A lower level of capacity is sufficient where the gift is insignificant in the context of the person's assets as a whole.

5:3.1 The nature of the transaction

A person making a gift should understand:

- that it is a gift, rather than, say, a loan or a mortgage advance or the acquisition of a stake or share in the recipient's business or property;
- whether he or she expects to receive anything in return;
- whether he or she intends the gift to take effect immediately or at some later date - perhaps on death;
- who the recipient is;
- whether he or she has already made substantial gifts to the recipient or others;
- whether the gift is a one-off or part of a larger transaction or series of transactions;
- the fact that, if the gift is outright, he or she will not be able to ask for the asset to be returned to them; and

- the underlying purpose of the transaction.

5:3.2 The effect of the transaction

The person making a gift should understand:

- the effect that making the gift will have on his or her own standard of living in the future, having regard to all the circumstances including his or her age, life expectancy, income, financial resources, financial responsibilities and financial needs; and
- the effect making the gift may have on the recipient.

5:3.3 The extent of the property

The person making the gift should understand:

- that the subject-matter of the gift belongs to him or her, and that he or she is entitled to dispose of it; and
- the extent (and possibly the value) of the property comprised in the gift in relation to all the circumstances and, in particular, in the context of his or her other assets.

5:3.4 The claims to which the giver ought to give effect

The person making the gift should be able to comprehend and appreciate the claims of the potential beneficiaries under his or her will or intestacy. For instance:

- the effect the gift could have on other beneficiaries;
- why the recipient is more deserving than others. For example the recipient may be less well-off financially, have devoted more time and attention to caring for the person, in need of greater assistance because of age, gender, or physical or mental disabilities;
- whether it is necessary to compensate others, perhaps by making a new will;
- did the person show any bias or favouritism towards the recipient before making the gift?

5:4 Gifts made by attorneys

An attorney acting on behalf of the donor of an enduring power has limited authority to make gifts provided that (a) there is nothing in the power itself which prohibits the attorney from making gifts and (b) the value of each gift is not unreasonable having regard to all the circumstances and, in particular, the size of the donor's estate. Attorneys can only make gifts to:

- a charity to which the donor made gifts, or might be expected to make gifts if he or she were not mentally disordered; or

- any person (including the attorney) who is related to or connected with the donor, provided that the gift is of a seasonal nature, or made on the occasion of a birth or marriage, or on the anniversary of a birth or marriage.

These rules apply regardless of whether the enduring power of attorney is registered or unregistered, but an attorney cannot make gifts (unless authorised to do so by the Court of Protection) while the power is in the course of being registered. If the power is registered and the attorney wishes to make more substantial gifts or gifts to people who are not related to or connected with the donor, or on an occasion other than a birth or marriage or birthday or wedding anniversary, he or she should apply for a direction from the Public Trust Office or an order of the Court of Protection (see also sections 3:2 and 5:5).

5:5 Gifts made on behalf of Court of Protection patients

Where a gift, or loan, or any other financial transaction in which there is a gift element is proposed on behalf of a patient for whom a receiver has been appointed:

- gifts which the patient can afford (because they come from surplus income or capital and are insignificant in the context of his or her assets as a whole) up to a ceiling of £15,000, are usually considered and allowed by the Public Trust Office on an application by letter only. In other words, no attendance at Court nor the issue of a formal application is necessary; or

- if the proposed gift does not fall within the above parameters, a formal application must be made to the Court of Protection. A hearing will be arranged and the Court will allow or prohibit the gift after considering all the evidence.

6 Capacity to Litigate

6:1 The test of capacity

The legal test for capacity to sue or be sued is whether that person has capacity to manage and administer his or her property and affairs (see section 3:2). The particular procedures to be followed when a person who is or may lack capacity is involved in litigation depends on the type of proceedings. The relevant procedural rules (which are presently under review) are contained in:

- Rules of the Supreme Court, Order 80;
- County Court Rules, Order 10;
- Family Proceedings Rules 1991, Part IX; and
- Insolvency Rules 1986, Part 7, Chapter 7.

These state that, where a person is incapable, by reason of mental disorder, of managing and administering his or her property and affairs (referred to as a "patient"), legal proceedings can only be conducted in his or her name and on his or her behalf by (a) a "next friend" where the person without capacity is bringing the proceedings; or (b) a "guardian ad litem" where the person without capacity is defending or responding to the proceedings.

Although the basis for assessing whether someone is capable of bringing or defending proceedings is the same as for the appointment of a receiver in the Court of Protection, a person without capacity who is involved in litigation does not automatically have to become a Court of Protection patient. Nevertheless, in important actions (for example: personal injury claims, proceedings relating to children, or the distribution of assets on a divorce) an application should be made to the Court of Protection for the appointment of a receiver if the litigant is without capacity.

A doctor who is asked to express an opinion on whether a person is capable of bringing or defending court proceedings should assess whether the person is:

(a) suffering from mental disorder; and

(b) incapable, by reason of that mental disorder, of managing and administering his or her property and affairs (see section 3:2).

6:2 The role of the Official Solicitor

The Official Solicitor performs a wide range of duties essentially based upon the representation of persons under a legal disability due to minority or mental disorder. The bulk of the workload consists in representing children and mental patients in a wide range of litigation. Perhaps the Official Solicitor's best known role is that of guardian ad litem of children in proceedings in wardship and under the Children Act 1989 and other family proceedings. This includes a number of cases where the permission of the court is sought for the child to undergo medical treatment (see section 10:5). Out of this has developed the Official Solicitor's role in adult medical consent cases (see section 10:4). The Official Solicitor will now usually be involved in all cases in which the giving or withholding of consent to medical treatment on behalf of an incapacitated patient is an issue. The patient is usually either a minor or an adult who is a patient within the meaning of Part VII of the Mental Health Act 1983, regardless of any actual capacity to instruct his or her own solicitor.

There are therefore a number of potential roles for the Official Solicitor. He or she may be the guardian ad litem of the person who is the subject of the proceedings, a defendant in his or her own right where proceedings might otherwise be without a defendant, or he or she may instruct counsel as amicus curiae. The Official Solicitor will always carry out impartial and independent enquiries to ensure that all relevant information is before the Court and all views are aired and expressed. When acting as guardian ad litem, the Official Solicitor is under a duty to supplement the lack of capacity of the subject of the proceedings; independent psychiatric and other medical evidence will frequently be commissioned. The Official Solicitor's functions and duties are more fully described in Practice Notes which are set out in Appendices D and E.

Early contact with lawyers in the Office of the Official Solicitor is advisable in those cases in which they are to be involved. Members of staff are always prepared to discuss cases over the telephone. The address and telephone number are given in Appendix C.

6:3 Out of hours applications to court

All cases in which the giving or withholding of consent to medical treatment is an issue are heard by judges in the Family Division of the High Court. Outside normal office hours, contact should be made, normally by counsel, with the security officer at the Royal Courts of Justice in London. He or she would contact the designated urgent business officer by telephone whose responsibility it would be to assess the urgency of the application and, if appropriate, to contact the Duty Judge. The Judge would, if necessary, contact the Official Solicitor. The Judge may grant the order sought over the telephone or may direct attendance at his or her lodgings. In the event of a medico-legal emergency, it is therefore prudent to have available to speak to the Judge both counsel and a relevant medical expert. A contact telephone number for the Royal Courts of Justice is included in Appendix C.

7 Capacity to Enter into a Contract

7:1 Introduction

It is difficult to generalise about an individual's contractual capacity. Without really being aware of it, most of us enter into some sort of contract every day. For example, purchasing groceries, buying a bus or train ticket, or depositing clothes at the dry-cleaners. However, some general rules apply to each of these contracts as well as to more complicated agreements with several pages of small print.

7:2 Specificity

The first rule is that contractual capacity relates to a specific contract, rather than to contracts in general. This means that a person could have capacity to buy a cinema ticket but not have the capacity to enter into a credit agreement with a mail order firm.

7:3 Nature and effect

The second rule is that a person must be capable of understanding the nature and effects of the specific contract. Obviously, the degree of understanding varies according to the kind of agreement involved. Some contracts (such as buying a pay-and-display ticket in a car park) require a relatively low degree of understanding, whereas others (such as a complex leasing agreement) demand a much higher level of understanding.

7:4 Voidable contracts

The third rule relates to what are known as voidable contracts. In dealing with contracts made by people lacking mental capacity the courts have had to counterbalance two important policy considerations. One is a duty to protect those who are incapable of looking after themselves, and the other is to ensure that other people are not prejudiced by the actions of a person lacking capacity who appears to be perfectly "normal". So, people without capacity will be bound by the terms of a contract they have entered into, unless it can be proved that the other party to the contract was aware of their mental incapacity. For example, at some stage a person suffering from hypomania is likely to go on a reckless shopping spree. If the shopkeeper has no reason to suspect that the customer is hypomanic, the customer will be bound by the contract, but if the shopkeeper was or should have been aware of the customer's mental state, the contract will be voidable (see section 7:6 for an exception).

7:5 Necessaries

The next rule concerns contracts for necessaries. A person with a mental incapacity who agrees to pay for goods or services which are necessaries is legally obliged to pay for them. "Necessaries" are defined in the Sale of Goods Act 1979 as goods which are suitable to the patient's condition in life and his or her actual requirements at the time of sale and delivery. Similar common law rules apply to services. Whether something is necessary or not is established in two stages. Firstly, it has to be decided whether, as a matter of law, goods or services are capable of being necessaries. Secondly, it has to be decided whether the goods or services were necessaries, given the particular circumstances of the incapacitated person who ordered them. The reference to goods being suitable to a patient's condition in life means his or her place in society, rather than any mental or physical condition.

Case law has established that goods will not be necessaries if the person's existing supply is sufficient. So, for instance, a patient who buys a pair of shoes would probably be bound to pay for them, but if the same patient purchased a dozen pairs, the contract might be voidable at the patient's option.

A contract for necessaries cannot be enforced against a person with a mental incapacity if it contains harsh or onerous terms. The Sale of Goods Act 1979 also provides that such a person is only required to pay a reasonable price for the goods. A reasonable price need not be the same as the sale price.

7:5.1 Proposals for law reform

The Law Commission has recommended a single statutory provision applying to the supply of both necessary goods and services to persons without capacity to contract for them.

7:6 Court of Protection patients

If someone comes under the jurisdiction of the Court of Protection because it has been established on medical evidence that he or she is incapable, by reason of mental disorder, of managing and administering his or her property and affairs, that person cannot enter into any contract which is inconsistent with the Court's powers (see section 3:2). Any such contract is void, even if the patient had contractual capacity when entering into it, even if the other party was unaware of the Court's involvement in the patient's affairs, and even if the contract was for necessaries (*Re Walker* and *Re Marshall*). However, the patient's receiver could apply to the Court for an order retrospectively approving the contract.

7:7 Checklist

If asked to express an opinion about someone's contractual capacity a doctor should discover information about:

(a) the specific contract to which the assessment of capacity relates; and

(b) whether the person is capable of understanding the nature and effect of that contract, for example:

- how much the person has to pay or is being paid;
- when the payment will be made or received;
- who the other party to the contract is;
- what is being given or received;
- any important terms and conditions which affect the person's rights and liabilities;
- whether the other party is aware of the person's possible incapacity.

8 Capacity to Vote

8:1 Entitlement to vote

The majority of people with mental health problems, whether caused by mental illness or learning disabilities, have the right to vote in Parliamentary and local elections. Greater encouragement is needed to ensure that their names are entered on the electoral register, and that they are given every opportunity to exercise their right to vote. It is rare for doctors or lawyers to become involved in determining capacity to vote, but better knowledge of the legal position may serve to encourage more people to register and to vote. It is a widely held belief that any degree of learning disability or mental illness renders a person ineligible to vote. This is not true, but such a belief may result in learning disabled people or mentally ill people being excluded from the electoral register - which does disqualify them from voting.

The people entitled to vote as electors in Parliamentary elections in any constituency, or in local government elections are defined (in the Representation of the People Act 1983) as those:

(a) whose name appears on the electoral register; and

(b) who are resident there on the qualifying date (which depends on the date of the election); and

(c) who on that date, and on the date of the poll, are not subject to any legal incapacity to vote (age apart); and

(d) who are either Commonwealth citizens or citizens of the Republic of Ireland; and

(e) who are aged 18 or over on the date of the poll.

The main questions which determine whether a learning disabled or mentally disordered person can vote are whether he or she is subject to any legal incapacity to vote and has a place of residence for voting purposes.

8:2 Legal incapacity to vote

Legal incapacity to vote was defined in a case in 1874 called *Stowe v Joliffe* as "some quality inherent in a person, which either at common law, or by statute, deprives him of the status of Parliamentary elector". This definition still applies today. In relation to mental capacity, the common law applies, and refers back to cases decided in the 18th century. For example, in 1785 in the *Bedford County Case, Burgess' Case* it was held that the name of an "idiot" (now presumably a severely learning disabled person) may not appear on the electoral register, and hence such a person cannot vote. In 1791, case law clarified that a "lunatic" (now presumably a mentally ill person) can vote, though only during a lucid interval (*Oakhampton Case, Robin's Case*). This view was confirmed in subsequent cases such as *Bridgewater Case, Tucker's Case*, with the result that mentally ill people should not be excluded from the electoral register.

While the terms referred to above are offensive and have no modern clinical application, the common law still applies in determining whether someone has the capacity to vote. However, it is the degree of mental incapacity which is relevant in deciding whether a person's name can be entered on the electoral register, and whether they can vote.

There is no definition in either statute or case law of the capacity to vote. The common law sets the threshold of understanding quite low, requiring only a capacity to understand in "broad terms" the nature and effect of voting and an ability to make a choice between candidates.

8:3 Eligibility for registration

There are no provisions in law which control the registration of electors of people who have a learning disability or mental illness and who are living in the community (as opposed to living in a hospital). In practice, the decision as to whether a learning disabled person is registered will be made by that person's carer by deciding whether or not to include the name of the disabled person on the electoral registration form (Form A) which is sent to all households in October of each year. This form does not raise questions of mental capacity, so there is no reason why all adults resident in the household should not be included, unless it is clear that a person lacks the capacity to make any sort of choice because of profound learning disability. The final decision as to whether a person's name is included in the electoral roll rests with the Electoral Registration Officer (ERO) who must consider each case on its merits. There is no requirement to obtain a medical opinion although the ERO may decide that a medical opinion would be helpful in determining a person's capacity to vote.

Recent guidance issued by the Home Office *Electoral Registration of Mentally Ill or Learning Disabled (Mentally Handicapped) People* which accompanies *Code of Practice Note No 5* (RPA 379) advises EROs to err, if at all, on the side of inclusion, rather than exclusion, in order to encourage people who have a degree of mental impairment to exercise their right to vote. This places the onus on people who wish to object to the inclusion of a name to make their case, rather than require learning disabled people who may be eligible to vote to use the appeals procedure in order to be registered.

8:3.1 Place of residence

There are special rules relating to the voting rights of patients in "mental hospitals", as such hospitals cannot be used as a place of residence for the purpose of electoral registration. The definition of mental hospital includes psychiatric and mental handicap hospitals and mental nursing homes, but not hostels or other residential care homes where the treatment of residents is not the primary purpose. The definition also excludes psychiatric wards of district general hospitals and homes for elderly people.

Voluntary (informal) patients in mental hospitals may continue to be registered for electoral purposes at their home address. However if their stay in hospital is so long that they have lost their residence, they may still register as electors, but only by completing a "patient's declaration" without assistance (unless they need help because of blindness or physical disability). The declaration must be attested (witnessed) by an authorised member of the hospital staff. Voluntary patients completing the declaration can use an address where they would be resident if they were not in hospital, or where they have lived in the past.

A person who is registered as an elector and who subsequently becomes a detained patient is eligible to vote during the currency of the register, unless he or she is subject to the common law incapacity to vote. Patients who are compulsorily detained in mental hospital under the Mental Health Act 1983 cannot be regarded as being resident at an address outside the hospital, and therefore are unable to register as electors.

It is for EROs to decide which hostels or residential care homes for elderly, mentally ill or learning disabled people come within the definition of a "mental hospital", if necessary after obtaining advice from the Department of Health or local health authority. For those hostels or homes which are not "mental hospitals", the ERO must decide which residents are entitled to be registered, if necessary with medical advice. The Home Office guidance mentioned above stipulates that the warden or person in charge of the home should not be asked to make a judgment as to which residents have the mental capacity to vote, as such a practice is not only objectionable in principle, but also open to abuse.

8:4 At the polling station

Any person whose name appears on the electoral register should be allowed to cast his or her vote unless, at the polling station on the day of the poll, it appears to the presiding officer that the elector may be so mentally incapacitated as to not have the common law capacity to vote. The presiding officer may put to the elector certain statutory questions permitted by the election rules. The permitted questions are:

(1) "Are you the person whose name appears on the register as... ?"
(2) "Have you already voted?"

Although these questions are inappropriate for determining mental capacity, no further questions may be put. If the presiding officer considers that the questions are not answered satisfactorily, he or she can refuse to issue a ballot paper.

Electors who are unable to read can ask the presiding officer to help them by marking their votes on the ballot paper, but they must be capable of giving directions to the presiding officer as to how they wish to vote. Otherwise, unless the elector is blind, no-one is allowed to accompany an elector into the polling booth or give any other assistance in marking the ballot paper.

8:5 Postal and proxy voting

The Representation of the People Act 1985 contains provisions for permitting an elector to vote by post or by appointing a proxy to vote on his or her behalf. No definition is given as to the mental capacity required to appoint a proxy, but it is presumed that the elector should have the common law capacity to vote. However, in order to appoint a proxy the elector must satisfy the requirements for postal voting. EROs will be able to explain the procedures and provide the relevant application forms. A separate application must be made for each election.

8:6 Conclusion

It is important that voluntary patients in hospital and residents in hostels and residential care homes are aware of their voting rights, and staff should assist them by providing information, declaration forms and absent voting forms, and by attesting declarations. The Home Office guidance (see section 8:3) stresses that the Department of Health, local health authorities and NHS trusts have a primary role in relation to voluntary patients. People with mental health problems living in the community will require help from their relatives, carers and sometimes their doctors to ensure they are not deprived unnecessarily of this most basic of civil rights.

9 Capacity to Enter Personal Relationships

9:1 Right to form relationships

Every person has fundamental rights which may not be infringed unless there are special and widely agreed grounds justifying such an infringement. Respect for individual rights in those matters which people can decide for themselves is embodied in national and international agreements. The United Nations Declaration on Human Rights of 1948, for example, articulates the rights of adults to freedom and equal treatment. Article 12 of the European Convention on Human Rights of 1951 provides "Everyone has the right to respect for his private and family life... men and women of marriageable age have the right to marry and to found a family, according to the national laws governing the exercise of this right". A balance must be maintained, however, between respecting individual rights to sexual relationships, marriage and parenthood and the duty of society (parents, carers and others) to protect vulnerable people and people with disabilities. In this context, judgments about capacity are extremely important and must be made with the aim of enabling all people to make their own decisions wherever possible.

Insofar as the right of mentally disordered people to enter into sexual relationships is concerned, the focus of the current law is not with their capacity to consent to such relationships but with protecting them from potentially abusive relationships. However, the relevant provisions of the criminal law are considered in this chapter, even though they are not strictly about capacity, in order to inform doctors and remind lawyers of the role which the criminal law plays in protecting vulnerable people, including those who may lack capacity, from abuse (see sections 9:3.1 and 9:3.2).

9:2 Capacity to consent to marriage

People with mental illness or learning disability (mental handicap) may marry if they have a broad understanding of what marriage is. The marriage ceremony requires both parties to enter into a contract. Capacity to do this was considered by the courts in a number of cases in the 1870s and 80s. In the case of *Hunter v Edney*, Sir James Hannen made the following statement about marriage, distinguishing between marriage and the wedding ceremony itself. He said, "the question which I have to determine is not whether she was aware that she was going through the ceremony of marriage, but whether she was capable of understanding the nature of the contract she was entering into".

9:2.1 Level of understanding required for marriage

The degree of understanding required in order to have capacity to enter into the marriage contract was considered in the case of *Durham v Durham* in which Sir James Hannen also said "the contract of marriage is a very simple one which does not require a high degree of intelligence to understand. It is an engagement between a man and a woman to live together, and love one another as husband and wife, to the exclusion of all others." In a more recent case the level of understanding was expressed as a broad understanding of "the duties and responsibilities normally entailing to a marriage" (*In the Estate of Park, Park v Park*).

Where one of the parties lacks capacity to consent to marriage then the marriage will be either void or voidable. A void marriage means that it will be treated as though it had never taken place and a voidable marriage is one which can be annulled at the request of one of the parties. A marriage will be **void** for lack of capacity to consent if it took place before 1st August 1971. A marriage will be **voidable** for lack of capacity to consent if it took place after 1st August 1971.

9:2.2 The effect of mental disorder

Under the Matrimonial Causes Act 1973 a marriage is voidable if at the time of marriage either party, although capable of giving valid consent, was suffering (whether continuously or intermittently) from mental disorder within the meaning of the Mental Health Act 1983 of such a kind or to such an extent as to be unfitted to marriage (see section 3:2.2 for the definition of mental disorder). The mental disorder may be of the petitioner or the respondent and to succeed the petitioner must show that the person's mental disorder made him or her incapable of living in a married state and carrying out the duties and obligations of marriage. However, merely being difficult to live with will not make a person unfitted to marriage (*Bennett v Bennett*). This provision of the Matrimonial Causes Act is not strictly a "capacity test".

Proceedings must be started within three years of the marriage, although the court may give leave for proceedings to be instituted at a later date. The court may not grant a decree in the case of a voidable marriage if the petitioner, knowing the marriage could be avoided, had acted in such a way that the respondent reasonably believed an annulment would not be sought and it would be unjust to grant a decree. A doctor asked to give an opinion about such an application should consult with those who know the party who is alleged to be mentally disordered and who have professional experience of the mental disorder.

9:2.3 What objections can be raised to a proposed marriage?

Sometimes a relative or carer of a person with a learning disability is concerned about a proposed marriage. There are a number of ways in which an objection to a pending marriage can be made. A person can:

- dissent from the publication of banns in the case of a church wedding;
- enter a caveat against the granting of a special or common licence; or
- enter a caveat with a superintendent registrar or the Registrar-General (in the case of a registry office wedding).

If a caveat is entered this puts the registrar or clergyman on notice and creates a requirement to investigate and enquire into the capacity of both parties to marry. The burden of proof of lack of capacity falls on the person seeking to oppose the marriage. The registrar may ask for a doctor's report or a report from a social worker, a psychologist or other person who can give information about the ability of the parties to understand the contract of marriage. The tests to be applied are those stated above (section 9:2) and it is important that a full consultation with all relevant people takes place. Any opinion should be based on a sound knowledge of the person, his or her way of life and any relevant religious or cultural facts. It is not necessary for the person to appreciate or consider every aspect of a marital relationship. See section 9:2.1 for case law on the level of understanding required.

When one or both parties proposing to marry has a learning disability it may be important to suggest counselling and to seek advice about the practical aspects of marriage including financial, housing and legal matters. Information and advice about sexuality and relationships including contraception may be useful, and should be made available. A judgment about the person's capacity to be a parent should be considered here and the possibility of future proceedings under the Children Act 1989 should be considered.

9:3 Consent to sexual relationships

Entering into a relationship is a personal decision which does not require any formal contract or test of capacity. Men and women can give legal consent to a heterosexual relationship at age 16 and men can consent to a homosexual relationship at age 18. The relationship can be of any duration and of varying degrees of intensity and commitment. Sexual relationships are also a matter of personal choice, so that if individuals are incapable of making the decision, no-one else may make it for them. The common law test of capacity to consent to sexual relations follows the usual form, that the person concerned:

(a) must be capable of understanding what is proposed and its implications; and

(b) must be able to exercise choice. (It is important to consider whether one party is in a position of power which will influence the ability of the other party to consent.)

For people with a learning disability there may be attempts by relatives and/or carers to stop the relationship because of concerns about pregnancy, the existence of a sexual relationship and risks of infection, and possible future marriage and/or parenthood. Doctors may be asked to give a view about the appropriateness of two people embarking on a close relationship and there may be concern about the ability of one or both parties to consent to sexual intercourse. It is important that the doctor should see the person privately to assess and advise on capacity.

9:3.1 General criminal laws which may be important

An awareness of possible criminal offences affecting all people may be important when advising and educating people with learning disability about their own sexuality and acceptable sexual behaviour. It is also important that the criminal law is enforced when people with learning disability/mental handicap are victims of sexual abuse and are exploited sexually by others (see section 9:4). The following criminal offences may be relevant:

Rape — Sexual intercourse between a man and a woman without the woman's consent will be rape. It is rape for a man to have intercourse with a girl or woman who does not have the capacity to understand the implications of what is taking place (*R v Howard*). If the man has a learning disability, and does not have the capacity to understand that the woman has not given her consent, he may not be held to be criminally responsible. Since 1994 it has also been recognised in law that a man can be raped.

Indecent assault — This can be committed on either a man or a woman and includes touching of an indecent nature and with an indecent motive. (Examples include touching breasts, genitals and other intimate touching without the consent of the person.) Neither men nor women who are severely mentally impaired can in law give consent to an act which, in the absence of valid consent, will be an indecent assault. A man who is assessed to have a "severe mental impairment" cannot in law consent to a homosexual act in private. This includes buggery and gross indecency.

Buggery — It is a criminal offence to commit buggery (anal intercourse by a man) with another person except between consenting men over the age of 18 in private.

Indecent exposure — This is an act against public decency in a public place and can be committed by a man or a woman (examples are masturbation or removal of clothes in public). It is not necessary to prove a sexual motive or intention to insult.

9:3.2 Specific criminal laws which may be important

There are a number of statutes which prohibit or impose limitations on the ability of people who are severely mentally impaired to give a valid consent to sexual intercourse. The aim of these provisions is to protect a severely mentally impaired woman from exploitation or abuse. For example, the Sexual Offences Act 1956 makes it an offence:

- for a man to have unlawful sexual intercourse with a woman who is "defective";
- to procure a woman "defective" to have unlawful sexual intercourse with any man or men;
- to take a "defective" woman away from the care of her parent with the intention that she shall have unlawful sexual intercourse with a man or men; and
- for "the owner, occupier or anyone who has, or acts or assists in the management or control of any premises to induce or knowingly suffer a woman who is a "defective" to resort to or be on those premises for the purpose of having unlawful sexual intercourse with men or with a particular man."

In this context the meaning of "defective" (now an obsolete and offensive term) is the same as the definition of severe mental impairment in the Mental Health Act 1983 (a state of arrested or incomplete development of mind which includes severe impairment of intelligence and social functioning), but without the need to show "abnormally aggressive or seriously irresponsible conduct", which is necessary for compulsory detention in hospital under the Act.

The Sexual Offences Act 1956 attempts to provide protection for women who are assumed, because of severe mental impairment, to be unable to consent to sexual intercourse. This assumption and the consequent unlawfulness of the act has the effect of inhibiting some relationships between adults with a learning disability/mental handicap. The law may also prevent carers and other staff from assisting and advising adults with a learning disability/mental handicap who wish to experience a sexual relationship to which they are capable of consenting.

There are other statutory offences which are intended to protect people with learning disability from sexual abuse and exploitation. For example:

- It is an offence for a man to have unlawful sexual intercourse with a woman suffering from a mental disorder if the man is the manager of, or on the staff of, a hospital or residential nursing home where the woman is an inpatient, or is an out-patient but on the premises. It is also an offence if the man is the guardian of the woman (Mental Health Act 1959).

- It is an offence for a male member of staff to commit acts of gross indecency on male patients (Sexual Offences Act 1967).

9:4 Protection from abuse or exploitation

People who are vulnerable (including learning disabled people, frail elderly people and people with mental illness) or those who may lack capacity must be protected from abuse and exploitation. Doctors and other carers attending residents or patients in institutional care have an important role in watching for and reporting the possibility of sexual abuse or exploitation. Where physical or sexual abuse is suspected or reported, it is advisable to inform the police immediately. This should be done with the consent of the person who appears to be suffering abuse and after explanations have been given about why it is important to inform other people. Where the alleged abuse is happening in a residential establishment, the registration authority should also be informed (this is a requirement of the Registered Homes Act 1984). If the person is unable or unwilling to consent to a police enquiry it may be necessary to report the matter to the police without consent if other residents are at risk or there are other important reasons. Bodies such as the General Medical Council and the British Medical Association give detailed guidance about the issues to be considered when achieving a balance between the confidentiality owed to the individual and the need to prevent foreseeable harm to that person or others. Each case must be carefully considered with the person making the allegations or the suspected victim.

9:4.1 Capacity to give evidence in criminal proceedings

It is important that all allegations of abuse are thoroughly investigated and criminal proceedings should be brought where this is possible. Some local authorities are now producing procedural guidelines concerning the actions to be taken in response to evidence of abuse of adults. People who are victims of alleged physical or sexual abuse will be important witnesses in a criminal trial. They will need to give evidence on oath in a public court and be subject to questioning and cross examination.

Unfortunately, there are many examples of failed prosecutions in cases of alleged physical and sexual abuse against vulnerable adults.

9:4.2 Victims as witnesses

The Crown Prosecution Service (CPS) may decide that a mentally vulnerable witness would not stand up to questioning in court and/or that there is insufficient evidence to secure a conviction. The CPS may also take the view that such a prosecution is not in the public interest. Lawyers acting for people who may lack capacity to take particular decisions should consider challenging decisions not to prosecute. It may be possible to provide support and advice to enable a learning disabled person to give reliable evidence. Sometimes an opinion of a doctor or other professional is sought by the CPS to attest to the capacity of the witness to take the oath in court and to give evidence. In this situation all the circumstances should be investigated before any opinion is given.

It is ultimately for the judge to decide whether a potential witness has capacity to take the oath in court and to give evidence, but the burden of proving this rests with the party calling the witness. Medical evidence as to capacity can sometimes be helpful, but there is doubt as to whether such evidence may be admitted. The judge must be satisfied, beyond reasonable doubt, that the potential witness:

(a) understands the duty to tell the truth; and

(b) understands the nature and consequences of taking the oath.

9:4.3 Who should advise on capacity in criminal proceedings?

The judge or the CPS may wish to seek expert opinions on the level of understanding of a particular witness. Reports may be provided by professionals with an understanding of mental disorder or mental handicap/learning disability. Those experts can include doctors, social workers, psychologists and others with professional qualifications and knowledge. Assessments of mental capacity should not be based of concepts of "mental age". When the "witness" or "suspect" is someone with a learning disability then a professional with particular knowledge of learning disability is essential. The appropriate expert may not necessarily be a doctor but could be a clinical psychologist or social worker.

9:5 Conclusion

It is important to remember the rights of people with disabilities or illness when considering their ability to make their own decisions. As noted above, the United Nations Declaration of Human Rights states that all adults are of equal value and have a right to the same freedoms. One of these rights for adults is the right to express their sexuality and to participate in family life.

10 Capacity to Consent to and Refuse Medical Treatment

10:1 Medical procedures

This chapter deals with capacity to consent to and refuse consent to medical procedures. "Medical procedures" means examination, diagnostic tests, and medical or nursing interventions aimed at alleviating a medical condition or preventing its deterioration. Therapies designed to rehabilitate patients are also included in this definition.

10:2 The need for patient consent

In most cases, health professionals cannot legally examine or treat any adult without his or her valid consent (the position of minors is dealt with in section 10:5). The principal exception is treatment provided under the Mental Health Act 1983. This authorises assessment of individuals, their admission to hospital or reception into guardianship and, if necessary, treatment for mental disorder. The treatment provisions of the 1983 Act are not discussed in detail in this book since they are well covered elsewhere (for example, the Mental Health Act Code of Practice (2nd edition 1993)). Apart from such compulsory treatment, it is unlawful and unethical to treat a person who is capable of understanding and willing to know, without first explaining the nature of the procedure, its purpose and implications and obtaining that person's agreement. Some people consent to treatment while *choosing* not to be told full details of their diagnosis or treatment. Their uninformed consent is nevertheless valid as long as they had the option of receiving more information.

10:3 Capacity to consent to medical procedures

As discussed in Part IV of this book, assessing capacity is a time-consuming exercise and some measures can enhance the perceived capacity of the person assessed. The legal presumption of capacity until the contrary is shown is important (see Part I). Assessing capacity to consent to medical treatment is somewhat different to other capacity assessments since the assessor may also be the person proposing the treatment. If the procedure proposed is a risky one or involves innovative techniques or if there is a divergence of opinion as to its benefits for the patient, additional safeguards are likely to be needed (see chapter 11 on research).

10:4 Adults

10:4.1 Adults' consent

The assessment of an adult patient's capacity to make a decision about his or her own medical treatment is a matter for clinical judgment guided by professional practice and subject to legal requirements. It is the personal responsibility of any doctor proposing to treat a patient to judge whether the patient has the capacity to give a valid consent. The doctor has a duty to give the patient an account in simple terms of the benefits and risks of the proposed treatment and explain the principal alternatives to it. The capacity required to make a decision about medical treatment was discussed in the case of *Re C (Adult: Refusal of Treatment)*. That case concerned whether a schizophrenic patient in Broadmoor Hospital had capacity to refuse consent to the amputation of his gangrenous foot. The High Court held that an adult has capacity to consent [or refuse consent] to medical treatment if he or she can:

(a) understand and retain the information relevant to the decision in question;

(b) believe that information; and

(c) weigh that information in the balance to arrive at a choice.

Therefore to demonstrate capacity individuals should be able to:

- understand in simple language what the medical treatment is, its purpose and nature and why it is being proposed;
- understand its principal benefits, risks and alternatives;
- understand in broad terms what will be the consequences of not receiving the proposed treatment;
- retain the information for long enough to make an effective decision; and
- make a free choice (ie free from pressure).

All assessments of an individual's capacity should be fully recorded in the patient's medical notes.

10:4.2 Adults' refusal

Competent adults have a clear right to refuse medical diagnostic procedures or treatment for reasons which are "rational, irrational or for no reason". This principle was established in the case of *Sidaway v Board of Governors of the Bethlem Royal Hospital and Maudsley Hospital*. The person's capacity to refuse in a valid manner must be assessed in relation to the specific treatment proposal. It is irrelevant whether refusal is contrary to the views of most other people if it is broadly consistent with the individual's own value system.

The principle that an adult patient has the right to refuse treatment as long as he or she has been properly informed of the implications and could make a free choice was affirmed by the Court of Appeal in the case of *Re T (Adult: Refusal of Treatment)*. That case concerned a 20 year old woman who was injured in a road traffic accident when she was 34 weeks pregnant. She had been brought up as a Jehovah's Witness and on admission to hospital refused a blood transfusion after having spent a period of time alone with her mother. T gave birth to a stillborn child after which her condition became critical. Her father and boyfriend applied for a court declaration that it would not be unlawful to administer a transfusion without her consent.

The Court of Appeal held that for such a refusal to be valid, doctors had to be satisfied that the patient's capacity to decide had not been diminished by illness, medication, false assumptions or misinformation, or that the patient's will had not been overborne by another's influence. In T's situation, it was held that the effect of her condition, together with misinformation and her mother's influence rendered her refusal of consent ineffective.

What is important about this case, notwithstanding the outcome for the individual patient, is the general affirmation of a patient's absolute right, properly exercised, to refuse medical treatment. Lord Justice Butler Sloss confirmed that:

> "A man or woman of full age and sound understanding may choose to reject medical advice and medical or surgical treatment either partially or in its entirety. A decision to refuse medical treatment by a patient capable of making the decision does not have to be sensible, rational or well considered ..."

A doctor's legal duties in relation to a patient's refusal of treatment were discussed in the same case when the Master of the Rolls stated:

> "Doctors faced with a refusal of consent have to give very careful and detailed consideration to the patient's capacity to decide at the time when the decision was made. It may not be the simple case of the patient having no capacity because, for example, at that time he had hallucinations. It may be the more difficult case of a temporarily reduced capacity at the time when his decision was made. What matters is that the doctors should consider whether at that time he had a capacity which was commensurate with the gravity of the decision which he purported to make. The more serious the decision, the greater the capacity required. If the patient had the requisite capacity, they are bound by his decision. If not, they are free to treat him in what they believe to be his best interests."

The Judge recommended that in cases of uncertainty doctors seek a declaration from the courts as to the lawfulness of treatment.

The clearest guidance so far from the courts on questions of capacity to consent to or refuse consent to medical treatment was set out in the case of *Re C (Adult: Refusal of Treatment)* (see section 10:4.1).

If an individual appears to be choosing an option which is not only contradictory to that most people would choose, but also appears to contradict that individual's previously expressed attitudes, health professionals would be justified in questioning in greater detail that individual's capacity to make a valid refusal in order to eliminate the possibility of a depressive illness or a delusional state. A specialist psychiatric opinion may be required. Practical aspects of assessment are discussed in Part IV of this book.

10:4.3 The incompetent adult

If an adult patient temporarily or permanently lacks capacity to consent to medical treatment no other person can consent to medical treatment on the patient's behalf. However, some forms of medical treatment will be lawful even in the absence of the patient's consent. The legal basis for carrying out a medical procedure in such cases is that the procedures are "necessary". In describing this exception to the general rule requiring patient consent (see section 10:2), the language of consent may be used, as consent in such circumstances can be implied or presumed or can be assumed will be obtained in the future.

10:4.3.1 The concept of necessity

The concept of "necessity" permitting doctors to provide treatment without obtaining the patient's consent was explained in the House of Lords in *Re F (Mental Patient: Sterilisation)* as justifying treatment where:

> "not only (1) must there be a necessity to act when it is not practicable to communicate with the assisted person, but also (2) the action taken must be such as a reasonable person would in all the circumstances take, acting in the best interests of the assisted person".

Although it is often assumed that the doctrine of necessity applies only to emergency situations, this is not the case. As defined by the Law Lords in *Re F (Mental Patient: Sterilisation)*, the doctrine of necessity permits:

> "action properly taken to preserve the life, health or well-being of the assisted person [which] may well transcend such measures as surgical operations or substantial medical treatment and may extend to include such humdrum matters as routine medical or dental treatment, even simple care such as dressing and undressing and putting to bed."

Not only is a doctor able to give treatment to an incapacitated patient when it is clearly in that person's best interests, it is a common law duty to do so. Nevertheless, this still only applies to treatment carried out to ensure improvement or prevent deterioration in health. If a person is now incapacitated but is known to have objections to all or some treatment (see section 10:6.2 on advance refusals) doctors may not be justified in proceeding, even in an emergency. If the incapacity is temporary because of anaesthetic, sedation, intoxication or temporary unconsciousness, doctors should not proceed beyond what is essential to preserve the person's life or prevent deterioration in health.

10:4.3.2 Best interests

The doctrine of necessity, which underpins treatment of people lacking capacity, is essentially made up of two components.

Firstly, there must be some necessity to act and secondly such action must be in the best interests of the person concerned. Under the current law the second limb of the necessity concept means that a doctor who acts in accordance with an accepted body of medical opinion will be acting in the best interests of the patient and will not be negligent in providing such treatment.

10:4.3.3 Treatment safeguards and procedures

Treatment decisions can be divided into broad categories not all of which require the involvement of a court.

(a) For most low-level decisions, there should generally be agreement between health professionals, people close to the patient and the incapacitated person (insofar as he or she can express a view) as to treatment. Simple treatment or diagnostic options such as the taking of samples for anaemia or lithium levels, the provision of a mild analgesic for a headache, antibiotics for an infection in an otherwise fit person are uncontroversial. The decision can be taken by the clinician, the patient and people providing care.

(b) Some treatment decisions are so serious that the courts have said that each case should be brought before the courts for independent review. Such treatments include non-therapeutic sterilisation (*Re F (Mental Patient: Sterilisation)*), and withdrawal of artificial hydration and nutrition from patients in a persistent vegetative state (*Airedale NHS Trust v Bland*). The High Court had held that its involvement is not necessary if a therapeutic operation will only have the incidental effect of sterilising a woman (*Re GF (Medical Treatment)*) or where termination of pregnancy is recommended (*Re SG (Adult Mental Patient: Abortion)*).

Other medical procedures are also likely to be so serious that they should be brought to the attention of the courts before they are carried out. Although there have been no court decisions on the matter it is likely that the courts would consider that they should be involved in decisions concerning tissue donation.

10:4.3.4 General principles

The following general principles should be taken into account when considering the medical treatment of a patient lacking capacity. The patient has a right to:

- be free from discrimination and should not be treated differently solely because of the condition that gives rise to the incapacity;
- privacy (The patient should be free from any medical procedures unless there are good therapeutic reasons for them. For example, questions are sometimes raised about subjecting non-sexually active incapacitated women to cervical cytology);
- confidentiality of personal health information;
- liberty (Patients should be free from interventions that inhibit liberty or the capacity to enjoy life unless such intervention is necessary to prevent a greater harm to the patient or to others. Appropriate justification must be shown for the use of restraints and it is inappropriate for restrictive measures to be used as an alternative to adequate staffing levels);
- dignity (The patient's social and cultural values should also be respected); and
- have his or her views taken into account even when they are considered legally incapable of determining what happens.

As a matter of good practice it is advisable to obtain a second opinion from another doctor in cases where a complex decision is contemplated. This can both assure the doctor proposing to treat the patient that the patient does lack capacity to consent and that the treatment is in the patient's best interests. It is recommended that for any serious procedure doctors should follow a series of basic steps including:

- considering whether there are alternative ways of treating the patient, particularly measures which might be less invasive;
- discussing the treatment with the health care team;
- discussing the treatment with the patient insofar as this is possible;
- considering any anticipatory statement of the patient's views;
- consulting other appropriate professionals involved with the patient's care in the hospital or community;
- consulting relatives and/or carers (see 10:4.3.5);

- obtaining a second opinion from a doctor skilled in the proposed treatment; and
- ensuring that a record is made of the discussions.

10:4.3.5 Views of relatives

Although it is currently unnecessary and of no legal effect to ask relatives to sign consent forms on behalf of their adult relatives who lack capacity, it has, nevertheless, long been accepted medical practice to consult people close to the patient to help the medical team assess what the patient would have wanted. In the case of *Re T (Adult: Refusal of Treatment)* the court held that the views of relatives are important insofar as they reflect what the patient would have chosen if in a position to decide.

10:4.3.6 Proposals for law reform

The Law Commission has recommended a significant overhaul of the law governing the treatment of people who lack capacity to consent to medical treatment. It recommends the introduction of a statutory authority for doctors to treat patients who are reasonably believed to lack capacity provided it is reasonable for the doctor to provide the treatment and the treatment is in the best interests of the person. The Commission has also recommended the introduction of new statutory safeguards for certain serious medical treatments including abortion, operations which will render a woman permanently infertile, tissue donation and the withdrawal of artificial nutrition and hydration from patients who are in persistent vegetative state.

10:5 Minors

10:5.1 Minors' consent

People under the age of majority (18 years) do not have the same rights at law as adults. Capacity, however, rather than age determines whether a child or young person can give legally valid consent to medical diagnostic procedures, examination or treatment. The legal ability of 16 and 17 year olds to give valid consent to surgical, medical and dental treatment was established by the Family Law Reform Act 1969. (Refusal of treatment, however, may be another matter: see section 10:5.2.) Thus, consent to medical treatment, (including voluntary treatment in a psychiatric hospital under the Mental Health Act 1983.) for mentally competent 16 and 17 year olds does not require reference to the patient's parents. Even prior to the Family Law Reform Act 1969 the general assumption was that consent by any minor who was sufficiently mature to understand the implications of treatment, would be valid. Many saw the 1969 Act, therefore, as freeing doctors from any doubt about the legal validity of consent in the over-16s and preserving the status quo for under-16s, for whom doctors would continue to make an assessment of maturity.

In the case of *Gillick v West Norfolk & Wisbech Area Health Authority*, the current legal position was established that minors of any age, who are able to understand what is proposed and have "sufficient discretion to be able to make a wise choice in their best interests" are competent to consent to medical treatment. No precise legal test for the capacity of children and young people, however, has been agreed. In the *Gillick* case, one view put forward implied that, in common with adult patients, the child patient was only required to understand the medical issues and purpose of the treatment. Another view put forward in the same case, however, was that the young patient should also understand the wider issues, such as the moral implications and the impact the decision may have on the family.

From the viewpoint of good practice, assessment of capacity should include consideration of the young person's:

- ability to understand that there is a choice and that choices have consequences;
- willingness and ability to make a choice (including the option of choosing that someone else makes treatment decisions);
- understanding of the nature and purpose of the proposed procedure;
- understanding of the proposed procedure's risks and side effects;
- understanding of the alternatives to the proposed procedure and the risks attached to them, and the consequences of no treatment; and
- freedom from pressure.

10:5.1.1 Views of parents

The views of parents are particularly important if the patient is very young or immature. In the case of *Re R (A Minor)(Wardship: Consent to Treatment)*, it was held that both minors and their parents have the legal power to consent to the medical treatment of the minor. A consent given by either, it was stated, is sufficient for treatment to proceed and only refusal by both parent and child would create a veto (see also the discussion of refusal at 10:5.2).

10:5.2 Minors' refusal

The courts have indicated that a refusal of treatment by a competent person under 18 can be overridden in law by parents or people with parental responsibility or by the High Court. Thus, where the views of a competent minor come into conflict with those of doctors and other people responsible for the minor, the law may intervene as a last resort. In the case of *Re R (A Minor)(Wardship: Consent to Treatment)*, the refusal of anti-psychotic treatment by a 15 year old ward of court was over-ruled. R was deemed incompetent but the Judge said that, even if she had been competent, R's refusal could still have been overruled. At the time of refusing medication, R appeared lucid and rational. The local authority which had previously consented on the girl's behalf to medication being administered to her, with-drew its consent in the face of her refusal. By so doing, the authority was acting in accordance with the principles established by the *Gillick* case (see section 10:5.1 on consent) that young people under 16, with sufficient maturity to make up their own minds could themselves legally consent to medical treatment. At the subsequent Court of Appeal hearing, it was confirmed that the court acting in wardship could overrule the decisions of a "Gillick competent" child as well as those of the child's parents or guardians.

The R case raised some uncertainty because of its interpretation of the principles established by *Gillick*. The Judge differentiated between powers to consent and powers to refuse treatment, stating that both minors and parents have powers to consent. The agreement of either, he said, was legally sufficient for treatment but only refusal of treatment by both parent and minor constitut-ed a veto. This appeared to contradict previous opinion, which assumed that the refusal of a competent child would be equally as valid as his or her consent and that the relevance of the parents' consent decreased in proportion to the increasing competence of the child.

Subsequently, in the case of *Re W (A Minor)(Medical Treatment: Court's Jurisdiction)*, a 16 year old anorexic patient was deemed competent but was overruled in her refusal of treatment. In this case, the patient's age might have been thought more persuasive as to the validity of her consent or refusal, since the Family Reform Act 1969 established that a 16 year old may consent as effectively as a person of adult years. That Act does not, however, address refusals of treatment. W was considered competent but her refusal of treatment for anorexia nervosa was overruled by the Court.

The Children Act 1989 gives a competent child the right to refuse medical or psychiatric examination or other assessment. But this too can be overridden by the court in certain situations as was shown by the case of *South Glamorgan CC v W & B*.

10:5.3 Consulting young people

Children and young people should be kept as fully informed as possible about their care and treatment. The individual's overall welfare should be the paramount consideration and listening to minors' views is conducive to promoting their welfare in the widest sense. They should also be encouraged to take decisions in collaboration with parents. If a minor refuses necessary treatment, however, parents or people with parental responsibility or the courts may legally authorise it.

Both national and international standards require that children and young people be consulted. The UN Convention on the Rights of the Child, for example, specifies that:

- the best interests of the child should be a primary consideration (Article 3);
- health services should be accessible to minors (Article 4); and
- the views of children and young people should be given due weight in accordance with their age and maturity (Article 12).

This right of participation in decision-making is given recognition in the Children Act 1989, which states that the views of children and young people should always be sought on any matter which affects them. Efforts should be made to explain the issues to them in a manner they understand in order to promote their cooperation.

10:6 Capacity to make anticipatory decisions

Adults who are capable of making current medical decisions for themselves can, if properly informed of the implications and consequences, also make anticipatory decisions about their preferences for medical treatment at a later stage when their capacity is impaired. Advance decisions cannot exceed those matters which a competent person can decide currently. Young people under the age of majority can make their wishes known but their wishes may not be determinative (see limits on minors' consent and refusal in sections 10:5.1 and 10:5.2).

10:6.1 Advance statements

Advance statements are declarations whereby competent people make known their views on what should happen if they lose the capacity to make decisions for themselves. Advance statements can take a variety of forms ranging from general lists of life values and preferences to specific requests or refusals. They can be written or oral. Their purpose is to provide a means for people to exercise autonomy by expressing an opinion in advance about future medical treatments. Individuals who are aware of a terminal illness or mental decline have often sought to discuss with their doctors how they wish to be treated. Advance statements enable a structured discussion and recording of the person's views to take place.

The test for capacity to make an advance statement about medical treatment is similar to that for capacity to make a contemporaneous medical decision. The treatment options, alternatives and implications of them should be broadly understood. Individuals should also be aware that circumstances and medical science may develop in unforeseen ways in the interval before their advance statement becomes operative. Also if the statement concerns a positive consent to or claim for certain treatments, the person making the statement should be aware that doctors are not legally bound by such a consent. Doctors cannot be compelled to carry out treatments which are contrary to their clinical judgment. The

BMA, together with the Royal Colleges and with the assistance of the Law Society, has published a detailed Code of Practice for health professionals on aspects of drafting, storage and implementation of advance statements which summarises accepted practice and the law.

10:6.2 Anticipatory refusals

A specific refusal of treatment is likely to be legally binding on health professionals if certain requirements are met. In case of uncertainty or dispute, courts may be asked to make a judgment as to the validity of the evidence of the person's intentions. A written, signed and witnessed refusal is likely to be convincing evidence of a settled wish and should be presumed to be valid in the absence of any indication to the contrary.

In the Court of Appeal, in the case of *Re T (Adult: Refusal of Treatment)*, it was held that an advance refusal of treatment by an adult would be legally binding if it is:

(a) clearly established;

(b) applicable to the current circumstances; and

(c) made without undue pressure from other people.

A clear and informed statement by a Jehovah's Witness refusing blood is an example of a potentially legally binding document. Any person making such a refusal should understand that the refusal of specific treatments may result in his or her death. Some advance refusals also specifically exempt health professionals from legal liability if they follow the individual's wishes in withholding or withdrawing treatment. In case of genuine doubt or ambiguity, however, as to the individual's intention or capacity at the time of drafting, health professionals should adopt a "best interests" approach until clarification can be obtained.

10:6.3 Limits on anticipatory refusals

The BMA has recommended that, as a matter of public policy, advance statements refusing basic care and maintenance of comfort should not be binding on health professionals. The BMA defines "basic care" very generally as "those procedures essential to keep an individual comfortable", such as pain and symptom relief (BMA Code of Practice on Advance Statements About Medical Treatment).

10:6.4 Proposals for law reform

The Law Commission has also stated that advance refusals cannot preclude the provision of basic care, which it defines as alleviation of pain, maintenance of cleanliness and provision of direct oral feeding. The Commission proposes specific legislation to clarify the current validity of advance refusals.

10:7 Confidentiality

All patients have rights to privacy and to control information about themselves. In the case of people with impaired capacity, however, the principle of confidentiality must be balanced with protection of their interests and, in very exceptional cases, the protection of others. Individual decision-making is always to be encouraged but inevitably carers and other people close to the individual lacking capacity will be involved in helping him or her to make decisions or in taking decisions on the individual's behalf. Increasing provision of care in the community means that more people have responsibilities in the provision of support for individuals lacking capacity. Nevertheless, unnecessary or widespread disclosure of identifiable personal health information without the individual's valid consent should not be a routine or automatic response.

Patients lacking capacity do not forfeit the right to control disclosure. They can authorise or prohibit the sharing of information about themselves if they broadly understand the implication of so doing. On the other hand, confidentiality is never absolute and, as with all patients, health professionals may have to consider breaching confidentiality, even in the face of a direct refusal by the patient, if there is a likelihood of foreseeable harm resulting from their silence.

Disclosure without consent should normally be restricted to the sharing of essential information with those who have a demonstrable need to know it in order to provide proper care and supervision of the individual. In exceptional cases, there may be justification for the disclosure of information to other people to whom the incapacitated person may represent a potential health hazard having first informed the patient of the intention to disclose. An example might be of a mentally incapable HIV-infected person embarking upon an intimate relationship. There can be no justification, however, of routine disclosure of that person's HIV-status to people whose contact with him or her contains no element of risk of infection.

As yet, there is no statute on the subject of confidentiality. In 1995, the statutory body for doctors, the General Medical Council, published the following statement:

"Disclosure in the patient's medical interests

Problems may arise if you consider that a patient is incapable of giving consent to treatment because of immaturity, illness or mental incapacity, and you have tried unsuccessfully to persuade the patient to allow an appropriate person to be involved in the consultation. If you are convinced that it is essential in the patient's medical interests, you may disclose relevant information to an appropriate person or authority. You must tell the patient before disclosing any information. You should remember that the judgment of whether patients are capable of giving or withholding consent to treatment or disclosure must be based on an assessment of their ability to appreciate what the treatment or advice being sought may involve, and not solely on their age.

If you believe a patient to be a victim of neglect or physical or sexual abuse, and unable to give or withhold consent to disclosure, it will usually be necessary to disclose information to an appropriate responsible person or statutory agency, in order to prevent further harm to the patient. In these and similar circumstances, you may release information without the patient's consent, but only if you consider that the patient is unable to give consent, and that the disclosure is in the patient's best medical interests.

Rarely, you may judge that seeking consent to the disclosure of confidential information would be damaging to the patient, but that the disclosure would be in the patient's medical interests. For example, you may judge that it would be in a patient's interests that a close relative should know about the patient's terminal condition, but that the patient would be seriously harmed by the information. In such circumstances information may be disclosed without consent."

10:8 Access to records

Under the Access to Health Records Act 1990, people have a statutory right of access to their own health records made after the Act came into force in November 1991. Parents can apply on behalf of immature children. Where a person has been deemed incapable of managing his or her property and affairs, access to the record can be given to any other person appointed by the Court of Protection to manage those affairs. (See section 3:2.1 on the Court of Protection.) In addition to the statutory provisions, health professionals have always exercised a discretionary ability to disclose information in the record to relevant people if they consider it would clearly be in the interests of the person lacking capacity to do so.

11 Capacity to Consent to Research and Innovative Treatment

11:1 Introduction

A person's capacity to consent to research is assessed in the same way as capacity to consent to medical treatment (see chapter 10). Additional safeguards, however, come into play if the research is non-therapeutic. Greater evidence of understanding is required if individuals are being asked to consent to their participation in something which brings them no likelihood of direct benefit. All research projects must be subject to the approval of a local research ethics committee (LREC).

11:2 Therapeutic and non-therapeutic research

Research procedures are generally divided into two categories, the distinction being based on the intention of the researcher.

(a) Procedures primarily aimed to benefit a particular patient but which incidentally also broaden knowledge of the condition or its treatment are classified as therapeutic research.

(b) Where the principal intention is to extend knowledge to benefit future patients, the research is non-therapeutic.

11:3 Research on adults

11:3.1 The competent adult

The consent of a competent adult to both therapeutic and non-therapeutic research must be based on appropriate information and level of understanding. In the context of non-therapeutic research, given the lack of intended benefit for the individual, courts are likely to limit the degree of risk an individual may assume. Some legal experts, for example, consider that courts would only accept as valid a competent person's consent to "minimal risk" procedures in this context, although the patient may validly consent to much greater degrees of risk if the intention is to achieve a benefit for him or herself by an experimental procedure.

81

11:3.2 The incompetent adult

Therapeutic research or non-therapeutic research which is not contrary to the interests of the incapacitated person, which exposes them to no or only minimal risk and which may benefit people in the same category may not be unethical but must be subject to careful scrutiny. It should be noted, however, that in the context of research involving pharmaceutical products the European Commission Guidelines on Good Clinical Practice for Trials on Medicinal Products effectively restrict research on subjects incapable of giving personal consent to that which "promotes the welfare and interest of the subject" (ie therapeutic research).

11:3.2.1 Therapeutic research

Where a patient lacks capacity to consent to his or her participation in therapeutic research no other person has the authority to give such consent on the patient's behalf (see section 10:4.3). This does not, however, mean that carrying out therapeutic research on a person lacking capacity is unlawful. The generally accepted view is that it is lawful for a doctor to carry out therapeutic research involving an adult who lacks capacity to consent provided that such research is in the patient's "best interests" as defined in *Re F (Mental Patient: Sterilisation)*.

11:3.2.2 Non-therapeutic research

Although the involvement of persons lacking capacity in non-therapeutic research is increasingly regarded as ethical provided certain safeguards are applied, it is doubtful that carrying out such research is lawful. The Law Commission's Report concludes (Law Commission Report 231, para 6.29):

> "If, however, the participant lacks capacity to consent to his or her participation, and the procedure cannot be justified under the doctrine of necessity, then any person who touches or restrains that participant is committing an unlawful battery. The simple fact is that the researcher is making no claim to be acting in the best interests of that individual person and does not therefore come within the rules of law set out in *Re F*".

11:4 Research on minors

Mature minors can give valid consent to medical examination, diagnostic procedures and treatment (see section 10:5.1). Their participation in research presents problems.

11:4.1 Therapeutic research

Minors who are considered to have capacity to consent to treatment can consent to research which is therapeutic and where the main aim is to benefit that individual. Although the consent of a mature minor may be sufficient from a general ethical viewpoint, doctors are advised to note the statements of the Medical Research Council (The Ethical Conduct of Research on Children) on the legal position. The MRC advises that:

> "When research projects involve young people between 16 and 18 years of age, particularly if there is some doubt as to the degree of understanding shown by the minor, it is good professional practice to seek the young person's permission to explain the research proposal to parents and, if the young person objects, to give these objections considerable weight.

> When minors are under 16 but have sufficient understanding and intelligence, they can consent to medical treatment and age is of no importance. Researchers, however, should be reticent to proceed without the approval of a parent or guardian and should certainly not do so without the prior agreement of the Local Research Ethics Committee (LREC)."

Legal advice issued by the Department of Health specifies that parental consent is required for participation in therapeutic research by minors under 16.

11:4.2 Non-therapeutic research

Both ethically and legally, non-therapeutic procedures involving minors are more difficult to justify. The validity of minors' consent will depend on their understanding and intelligence, the information provided, whether the consent is free from undue influence and the degree of risk or intervention involved. As with any non-therapeutic procedure the degree of understanding required must be commensurate with the seriousness and risks of the procedure. There is no clear legal requirement to consult the parents of a competent minor. Nevertheless, it would be wise to do so. Although the age of the minor should not be determinative, common sense indicates that the younger the child, the more desirable is parental involvement. Nevertheless, there is doubt as to whether even parents can give valid legal consent to non-therapeutic procedures on their children. In 1991, the Department of Health in its guidance "Local Research Ethics Committees" stated:

"Those acting for the child can only legally give their consent provided that the intervention is for the benefit of the child. If they are responsible for allowing the child to be subjected to any risk (other than one so insignificant as to be negligible) which is not for the benefit of the child, it could be said that they were acting illegally."

By definition, non-therapeutic research is not intended to favour the interests of the individual subject but it may not be contrary to the subject's interests. Research involving procedures contrary to the child's interests would be unethical and is likely to be judged unlawful. There appears to be a broad consensus that participation by immature minors in non-therapeutic research is not necessarily unethical as long as:

- the research carries no more than minimal risk;
- it does not entail any suffering for the child;
- parental and LREC agreement is obtained; and
- the child does not appear to object.

The law, however, is less clear on this issue and is likely to depend on the degree of risk or invasiveness of the procedures involved.

11:5 Innovative treatment

Innovative treatments are often an extension of usual treatments but they may expose the patient to a greater degree of risk than established procedures. An experienced surgeon, for example, may modify a particular surgical procedure for an individual patient if a superior outcome might be expected from the modification. Patients should be informed of how and why the proposed treatment differs from the usual measures and the known or likely risks attached. Innovative treatments are usually seen as a standard feature of medical practice and the fact that useful information is gained as a by-product is seen as largely incidental. Any test by "trial and error", however, obviously leaves patients vulnerable unless carefully monitored and subject to high standards of informed consent. In particular, exposing incapacitated patients to innovative therapies is likely to give rise to legal and ethical uncertainty. The BMA recommends that in any instance where a doctor proposes a procedure which diverges substantially from accepted practice, involving an unknown or increased risk, advance expert scrutiny of the ethics and legality of the procedure is desirable.

11:6 Proposals for law reform

The involvement of adults lacking capacity to consent to their participation in both therapeutic and non-therapeutic research has been under consideration by the Law Commission. The Commission considers that its proposed general authority to do what is reasonable and in the best interests of the patient would provide lawful authority for any doctor carrying out therapeutic research on persons lacking capacity (see Appendix A).

For non-therapeutic research the Law Commission has recommended that research which is unlikely to benefit a participant, or whose benefit is likely to be long delayed, should be lawful if (a) the research is into an incapacitating condition with which the person is or may be affected, and (b) certain statutory procedures are complied with. The statutory procedures referred to relate primarily to obtaining the approval of a new statutory committee.

PART IV

Practical Aspects of the Assessment of Capacity

12 Practical Guidelines For Doctors

12:1 Introduction

Capacity is a legal concept and the tests which are applied to determine whether a person has any particular capacity originate in law. Ultimately, the decision about a person's capacity can be decided by a court. In practice, however, doctors frequently give opinions about capacity which are accepted without further legal intervention. A doctor may be required:

(a) to make an assessment of capacity prior to medical treatment;

(b) to provide a "medical certificate", at a solicitor's request, as to a particular capacity unrelated to medical treatment;

(c) to witness or otherwise certify a legal document signed by someone;

(d) otherwise to give an opinion as to a particular legal capacity which is relevant to court proceedings.

Irrespective of whether the doctor is assessing the capacity to consent to medical treatment or a capacity which is unrelated to medical treatment, the doctor should make careful reference to the relevant legal criteria. The doctor should then assess whether the person's mental capacity is adequate to satisfy those criteria. It is important for doctors to recognise that there can also be non-medical evidence about a person's capacity, which may sometimes contradict their own medical view. This emphasises that the doctor's role is to give an opinion rather than to be the sole arbiter as to capacity. Any medical opinion about capacity is open to legal challenge, either by the person concerned or by some other interested party, and, ultimately, the doctor can be called to give evidence in court.

12:2 What is capacity?

An assessment of capacity is not based upon the test, "would a rational person decide as this person has decided?" It is not the decision itself but the thought process which lies behind the decision which is relevant to the question of capacity. Individuals who have mental capacity may make decisions which are apparently completely irrational and the law allows them to do so. There is a presumption both that a person has capacity until the contrary is proven and that a person who legally lacks capacity remains in that state until the contrary is proven (see section 2:2.1). Since the presumption of capacity must be the starting point of any assessment, lack of cooperation or apathy with respect to an assessment of capacity should not lead to a conclusion that the person lacks capacity. For example, the eccentric recluse must not lose legal autonomy simply because of non-cooperation with an assessment.

Existing legal tests of capacity do not necessarily look to whether there is a diagnosable medical condition. What is important is the ability of the person to pass the relevant test (see Part III for existing legal tests). Where there is a medical disorder, it is not the particular diagnosis which implies capacity or incapacity but, rather, the person's specific disabilities. Similarly, different legal capacities can be variously affected by a particular medical disability. A diagnosis of schizophrenia does not, of itself, determine whether or not a person lacks a particular capacity. For example, a person with schizophrenia may have the capacity to accept or refuse some medical treatments but not others, depending upon the nature of his or her disordered thoughts, perceptions or mood *(Re C (Adult: Refusal of Treatment))*. More generally, a person may have the capacity to carry out one type of legal act, such as marrying, whilst not having the capacity to carry out another, such as making a will.

A person's capacity will largely be determined by that person's mental state. However, there may also be some physical conditions which do not directly affect mental functioning but which can effectively interfere with capacity. Disabilities of communication may be relevant to whether a person's wishes can be ascertained. However, such communication problems can often be overcome.

The Law Commission has recently recommended (Law Commission Report No 231 (1995)) that its new test of capacity, except in cases where the person is unable to communicate, should require that a person's inability to make a decision is linked to the presence of a "mental disability" (a definition of this term is included in Clause 2 of the Law Commission's draft Bill which is set out in Appendix A). The arguments for and against such a diagnostic hurdle are very finely balanced and they are set out in full in the Law Commission's Consultation Paper No 128 (1993). There appears to be good reason to agree with the Law Commission's view that a diagnostic hurdle does have a role to play in any definition of incapacity, in particular in ensuring that the test is stringent enough not to catch large numbers of people who make unusual or unwise decisions.

12:3 The doctor's role

Although assessing any particular capacity does not require highly detailed legal knowledge, the doctor must understand in broad terms the relevant legal tests. The doctor's role is to supply information on which an assessment of the person's legal capacity can be based, that is, to describe the consequences of medical conditions which (may) compromise an individual's ability to pass the legal test. If there is no medical diagnosis there can be no relevant medical evidence as to capacity. For example, to say that a person "makes poor judgments" is not a medical opinion but a lay observation and, indeed, one which is heavily subjective. This emphasises the importance of the doctor first of all determining that it is appropriate to give a medical opinion about capacity.

Although the doctor may be asked to give an opinion about capacity, such an opinion is not necessarily the deciding factor. For example, the doctor may be of the opinion that the person is incapable of doing something but there may be evidence from other people which suggests otherwise. Also, some tests of capacity make explicit or implicit reference to social functioning rather than to medical disabilities *per se* and a doctor is no more expert in assessing social functioning than anyone else.

Where the relevant legal capacity is the capacity to consent to specific medical treatment doctors should take particular care. The doctor may be in a situation where his or her opinion of the patient's best interests conflicts with what the patient wants. It is tempting, but ethically and legally wrong, for the doctor to underestimate the capacity of the patient in order to achieve what the doctor believes to be in that person's best interests. In so doing the doctor deprives the patient of his or her autonomy.

12:3.1 Professional ethics

There are two distinct contexts in which doctors examine people. The most common is the therapeutic context to ensure that patients receive appropriate care and treatment. Patient consent is normally implicit, as is permission to disclose to other health professionals such information as is essential for the provision of care. Nevertheless, the BMA maintains that it is good practice to inform patients about the scope of disclosure within the therapeutic context, since care is increasingly provided by inter-disciplinary teams and information may be spread more widely than patients anticipate.

The second situation is where doctors act as independent examiners in order to provide a report for purposes other than treatment. When a doctor is carrying out this second type of assessment, patient consent to examination and to disclosure of information cannot be assumed. It is essential that the doctor's role and the purpose of the exercise is explained to the person at the outset. No-one can legally consent to examination on behalf of an adult but relatives may help ensure that the person understands the situation. It is easier for both sides to have clear expectations about the aim of assessment when the person examined is not the doctor's own patient.

Ensuring clarity is more complicated when assessment for a report to third parties takes place within the context of a continuing therapeutic relationship. In such cases, the doctor must explain how the examination differs from the usual doctor-patient encounter and obtain explicit patient consent. Patients must also be told who will have access to the information gained and whether other material from their past records will be needed. The patient's consent to such disclosure should be recorded.

If an individual appears competent and refuses to cooperate with assessment, the doctor must note that fact in conjunction with the other evidence available. If it appears likely that the person lacks capacity to consent to assessment or to disclosure, the doctor should take a decision based on a judgment of the person's "best interests". Such judgment necessarily includes appropriate weight being given to the ascertainable past and current wishes of that individual.

12:3.2 Which doctor should assess the person?

Many people can be assessed by their general practitioners. Indeed a close, long term acquaintance with the person being assessed may be an asset, particularly if that person is more relaxed with a familiar doctor. However, the general practitioner's personal knowledge of a patient, and perhaps also of the patient's family, may make an objective assessment more difficult. If the nature of the person's medical disorder or disabilities suggests that a hospital specialist is needed then it will be important for that doctor to obtain information from the general practitioner to make his or her own assessment of the patient's capacity.

12:4 A systematic approach to assessing capacity

Once sure of the relevant legal test, the assessing doctor should become familiar with any background information about the person likely to be relevant to that particular test. The amount of information required will be determined by the complexity of the legal decision to be taken. For example, if the assessment relates to the capacity to make a will, the assessing doctor will need to have some idea about the extent and complexity of the person's estate and whether the person understands the claims of others to which consideration should be given in deciding about disposal of his or her assets. The doctor must therefore have some knowledge of the number and nature of the claims on the individual (see chapter 4 on making a will). Although the medical assessment should be carried out with an eye to the relevant legal criteria, there must be a clear distinction between the description of the disabilities and the interpretation of how they affect legal capacity. The doctor should, therefore, first define the diagnosis and the medical disabilities and then assess how these affect the person's ability to pass the relevant legal test.

Prior to undertaking the assessment, the doctor should try to have access to all relevant past medical and psychiatric records. An understanding of the progression of the person's disease will be relevant to prognosis, to any likely response to treatment, and thus to future potential capacity. Assessment of the permanence or transience of disabilities may be crucially important in offering a view about achievable capacity. Also, the medical records may give a different picture of a person's disabilities in general terms from that which the doctor gains at an individual assessment and it is important for the doctor to make an assessment on the basis of all of the information available. It is also important for the doctor to take full account of relevant information from other disciplines. An assessment by a clinical psychologist may already be available, or could be sought, and this may assist in giving a detailed, validated and systematic assessment of cognitive functioning. An occupational therapist might properly be consulted when information about daily functioning is of importance. Also, a report from a nurse or from an approved social worker may sometimes be helpful.

Information from friends, relatives or carers is often of great importance in the assessment of disability and its progression. However, great care must be taken when gaining information from such third parties, particularly if they have an interest in the outcome of the assessment of capacity. It is also important to take account of the person's known previous patterns of behaviour, values and goals. These may give clues as to whether current behaviour and thinking reflects an abnormal mental state. Aspects of a person's current thinking may derive not from a medical disability but from a normal personality, or from a particular cultural or ethnic background, and this may be of great importance in determining capacity. It may even be necessary for the doctor to seek advice from others on such cultural issues, or to suggest that the patient be examined by a doctor of a cultural or ethnic background similar to the person being assessed.

Where the person suffers from a mental disorder, it is good practice to express the diagnosis in terms of one of the accepted international classifications of mental disorders, the World Health Organisation International Classification of Diseases (WHO ICD 10), or the American Psychiatric Association, Diagnostic and Statistical Manual (DSM IV). This will ensure greater diagnostic consistency between doctors and minimise diagnostic confusion.

12:5 The mental state in relation to capacity

Examination of the mental state is fundamental to the assessment of capacity. Although particular diagnoses may tend to be associated with particular mental state disabilities which affect capacity, what matters are the disabilities themselves. It is only through detailed assessment of specific aspects of mental functioning that capacity can be properly assessed. The following illustrates ways in which specific abnormalities in the mental state can affect capacity.

Appearance and behaviour — A patient may be so agitated or overactive in his or her behaviour that it may be impossible to impart relevant information. Otherwise, appearance and behaviour may suggest a mood disorder or cognitive abnormality which might be relevant to the person's capacity.

Speech — The rate, quantity, form or flow of speech may be such as to interfere with communication, as well as reflecting abnormality of thought processes. For example, a depressed patient may be so lacking in speech as to be unable to communicate effectively; or a hypomanic patient may make only tangentially linked utterances, perhaps at high speed, to the extent that communication is severely impaired. Similarly, the "knight's move" thinking of a schizophrenic patient (moving between topics without apparent logical connections) may make communication very difficult or even impossible. Damage to the language areas of the brain following a stroke may also make direct verbal communication impossible.

Mood — Mood may be very important in determining capacity. The depressed patient, seeing no future, may make decisions relevant to his or her affairs on an entirely erroneous and depressive basis. Similarly, the grandiose approach of a hypomanic patient may lead to rash financial or other decisions. Lability of mood, for example, following frontal lobe damage, may render a patient unable to make consistent decisions or unable to stick to decisions once they have been made. Anxiety will also often have some effect on the assessed level of capacity although, by itself, it will rarely lead to incapacity.

Thought — Abnormalities of thought may have a profound effect upon decision-making. Delusions which are strongly held, and which relate specifically to the decision at hand, may substantially distort a person's ability to make the decision. For example, a delusional belief that a close relative is plotting against him or her might affect that person's capacity to make a will. Similarly, a delusional belief that doctors have magical powers to cure may render the patient incapable of consenting to medical treatment. Thought abnormalities falling short of delusions, for example, extreme preoccupation or obsessional thoughts, can also interfere with capacity but are less likely to do so. Highly overvalued ideas falling short of delusions, such as occur in anorexia nervosa, present particular difficulties in relation to the capacity of such patients to consent to treatment or to accept or refuse food.

Perception — Illusions are rarely significant enough to inhibit capacity. Hallucinations, however, may well be of direct relevance to decision-making. They are often congruent with, or reinforce, delusions and so the two should be considered together. Auditory hallucinations instructing the patient may have two distinct effects. Firstly, by their content and authority they may directly interfere with the patient's ability to think about relevant issues as well as decision-making ability. Secondly, hallucinations may be so incessant that they distract the person from thinking about the decision at all. By contrast, organically determined hallucinations are very unlikely to interfere with capacity since patients generally know that they are not "real" (albeit they are perceived as such).

Cognition — Defects in cognition can have profound significance for capacity. Decision-making and all tests of legal capacity require not only consciousness but some continuity of consciousness and of recollection. Attention (the ability to focus on the matter in hand) and concentration (the ability to sustain attention) are necessary for effective thought and, therefore, for capacity. Patients who are highly distracted, whether by other mental events such as hallucinations or because of an organic brain disorder, may lack capacity.

Memory — Memory may be essential for logical manipulation of concepts. A person with a severe short term memory deficit, that is, an inability to recall information told to him or her a few minutes earlier (for example, as part of Korsakoff's psychosis as a result of chronic alcoholism) may lack capacity for some decisions. However, a long term memory deficit (memory of remote events) will not usually reduce capacity, so long as the information necessary for the decision does not arise from the long term memory store. Even if it does, it may be possible to give the patient the relevant information afresh and thus achieve capacity. Memory disturbance due to a hysterical dissociative mechanism will only affect capacity to make decisions which relate to events which are directly affected by the mental mechanism itself.

Intelligence — This relates to global cognitive function, summarised as performance abilities and verbal abilities. Very low intelligence (for example, from learning disability) may reduce capacity for certain decisions. However, great care should be taken not to presume incapacity just because the person is learning disabled. There should be careful investigation of the ability of the person specifically in relation to the decision in question. Acquired brain damage, whether from trauma or from disease processes affecting the brain, can also affect general mental functioning and, therefore, capacity. However, where only certain aspects of intellectual functioning are significantly damaged it is important to be very specific in distinguishing which functions, or combination of functions, are necessary for the legal capacity which the person must have. Standardised psychometric tests may be of help in defining cognitive disabilities.

Orientation — Awareness of time, place and person, might be seen as tending only to set the context for decisions rather than being directly relevant to decision-making. However, disorientation is usually a marker of severe brain dysfunction, such as occurs in acute confusional states and dementia, and other aspects of these conditions may well inhibit capacity.

Insight — People can lack insight into one aspect of their lives and retain it for others. For example, lack of insight as to the presence of illness might not deprive a person of the capacity to make decisions about the treatment of the illness if the person has insight into the need for such treatment. Furthermore, insight may not be completely absent. The person with reduced insight may have specific awareness of his or her condition so as to have the capacity necessary for decisions about treatment. Of course, lack of insight into mental illness may not inhibit the person's capacity to decide about something else in his or her life. No report should read "has insight" or "has no insight"; either is, unqualified, a valueless statement.

12:6 Personality disorders

By contrast with mental illness or organic brain syndromes, personality disorders present particular problems in relation to capacity. Such patients (often with a diagnosis of "borderline personality disorder" or "psychopathic personality disorder") have disorders which are all-pervasive of their mental and social functioning, as well as of their behaviour. They often experience profound mood disturbances or swings and are also often very impulsive. Their thoughts are usually highly disordered but they are not deluded. It is the manner in which they weigh decisions in the balance which is generally affected, not the ability to think *per se*. Assessment of capacity in such patients is extremely difficult since there are no clear-cut profound abnormalities in the mental state (such as those described above) and yet the doctor will often perceive that they are not making decisions in the way that an ordinary person would. There should be no automatic assumption that this necessarily indicates impaired capacity.

12:7 The duty to enhance mental capacity

Doctors should be aware both that medical disabilities can fluctuate and that there are many factors extraneous to a person's medical disorder which may adversely influence capacity. It is the duty of the assessing doctor to maximise capacity. The following points may assist.

- Any treatable medical condition which affects capacity should be treated before a final assessment is made.

- Incapacity may be temporary albeit for a prolonged period. For example, an older patient with an acute confusional state caused by infection may continue to improve for some time after successful treatment. If a person's condition is likely to improve, the assessment of capacity should, if possible, be delayed.

- Some conditions, for example, dementia, may give rise to fluctuating capacity. Thus, although a person with dementia may lack capacity at the time of one assessment, the result may be different if a second assessment is undertaken during a lucid interval. In cases of fluctuating capacity the medical report should detail the level of capacity during periods of maximal and minimal disability.

- Some mental disabilities may be untreatable and yet their impact can be minimised. For example, the capacity of a person with a short term memory deficit to make a particular decision may be improved if trained in suitable techniques by an occupational therapist or psychologist. If the assessing doctor believes that capacity could be improved by such assistance then this should be stated in any opinion.

- Some physical conditions which do not directly affect the mental state can *appear* to interfere with capacity. For example, disabilities of communication may not reflect an inability to understand relevant information or make a choice but may simply reflect an inability to communicate the person's wishes. Many communication difficulties which result from physical disabilities can be overcome and this emphasises the importance of recognising the true basis of what is only an apparent incapacity. There should, therefore, be careful assessment of speech, language functioning, hearing and (if appropriate) sight. Any disabilities discovered should, as far as possible (and if time allows), be corrected before any conclusion is reached about capacity.

- Care should be taken to choose the best location and time for the assessment. In someone who is on the borderline of having capacity, anxiety may tip that person into apparent incapacity. It may be appropriate to assess the person in his or her own home if it is thought that an interview at either a hospital or a GP's surgery would adversely affect the result. A relative or carer may be able to indicate the most suitable location and time for the assessment.

- The way in which someone is approached and dealt with generally can have a significant impact upon apparent capacity and the doctor should be sensitive to this.

- Educating the person being assessed as to the factors relevant to the proposed decision may enhance capacity. Indeed, the assessing doctor should always establish what the person understands about the decision he or she is being asked to undertake. It is important for the doctor to re-explain and, if necessary, write down those aspects of the decision which have not been fully grasped. The person being assessed should be allowed sufficient time to become familiar with concepts relevant to the decision. For example, people with learning disabilities may have difficulty in consenting to sexual relationships if they are ignorant about issues relating to sexuality and abuse. With a careful explanation of the relevant issues such people may be capable of consenting to personal and sexual relationships.

- The capacity of some people may be enhanced by the presence of a third party at the interview. Alternatively, the presence of such a person may increase the anxiety and thus reduce the capacity of the person. The person being assessed should be asked specifically whether he or she would feel more comfortable with some friend or other person present.

- Depression is common amongst those with other disabilities but is often not recognised. Its presence may profoundly affect capacity and yet it may be amenable to treatment. Making a diagnosis of depression in the presence of other disabilities affecting mental functioning can be particularly difficult, especially in patients with dementia. The opinion of a psychiatrist may be necessary in such cases. The low self-esteem of many patients whose capacity may be in question means that they are at particular risk of "going along with propositions" regardless of their own private views. The assessing doctor should be aware of this and structure the interview so as to avoid the use of leading questions.

12:8 Retrospective assessment

On occasions a doctor may be asked to advise whether a person had the capacity some time in the past to make a decision which was made. An example might be the capacity to make a will (where the person has subsequently died). Any such retrospective assessment will have to be based upon medical notes made at the time, as well as on other non-medical information which suggests the nature of the person's mental functioning at the time.

12:9 General guidance

Assessment of capacity is not a function which can usually be carried out in only a few minutes. Aside from situations where the patient is comatose, or otherwise so severely disabled that incapacity is obvious, assessment will usually take a substantial period of time. This is required both because of the need to be thorough and comprehensive and because of the legal importance which attaches to the assessment. The doctor should never be constrained in making assessment by time or resources. Each assessment of capacity must be an assessment of an individual in his or her own circumstances. No assumptions should be made about capacity just on the basis of the person's known diagnosis. What matters is how the medical condition affects the particular person's own capacity, not the diagnosed medical condition itself.

It is worth emphasising again that the doctor must guard against allowing a personal view of what is in the person's best interests to influence an assessment of capacity. It may be disconcerting for the doctor to determine that the patient has capacity when the doctor believes that allowing the patient to make the decision will be against the patient's long term interests. However, the doctor must not consider the implications of the person being allowed to make the decision except to the extent that this is relevant in deciding whether the person has the capacity to do so.

13 Practical Guidelines for Lawyers

13:1 Introduction

Lawyers should be clear about which kind of doctor to ask to give an expert opinion about any particular legal capacity. They should also clarify for the doctor the relevant legal test(s) of capacity and describe the client's circumstances. It is often helpful for there to be a discussion between lawyer and doctor prior to the doctor's consideration of the case, both to clarify the legal questions and to establish what documentary information is available and which the doctor should see. It would also be helpful for lawyers to have some knowledge of the basic medical principles which underlie the assessment in order both to evaluate the opinion and to be sure of understanding its legal implications. This chapter attempts to offer basic information about different specialties and medical personnel, and about the nature of psychiatric assessment and diagnosis.

13:2 Who should assess the person?

Doctors should not assess a person's capacity from the standpoint of their medical professional skill other than where the person suffers (or may suffer) from a diagnosable medical condition. Lawyers should therefore guard against any assessment which appears to be "medical" but which has nothing to do with medical disabilities.

Mental disabilities can arise from either "medical" or "psychiatric" conditions. However, any doctor should be able to take a psychiatric history and to conduct a basic mental state examination, in order to define straightforward abnormalities irrespective of their diagnostic cause. Where the person's capacity is borderline and the disabilities and their interaction with the legal tests of capacity are complex it may be appropriate to seek a specialist opinion.

13:2.1 Specialty knowledge

Hospital medicine is divided into specialties. Some patients with a possible legal incapacity will require assessment by a psychiatrist. This is a doctor who is trained to assess and treat all disorders which can present with psychiatric or mental symptoms. Hence, both "organically" (physically) and "functionally" (non-organically) caused illnesses can present with mental symptoms. For example, a patient complaining of "voices" might have either schizophrenia or a particular sort of epilepsy. This emphasises the importance of the primary diagnostic decision being taken by a medical practitioner (by contrast with a clinical psychologist) if there is any possibility that the condition may be organically caused. Once the diagnosis is clearly established as "organic" it may be appropriate for the patient's condition to be treated, or capacity assessed by a non-psychiatric specialist (for example a neurologist). It is important to choose a specialist based not so much on the specialist's detailed research knowledge but upon his or her clinical acquaintance with the condition and experience of caring for patients with that condition. Hence, a psycho-geriatrician may be a better "expert" on Alzheimer's Disease than a research neurologist. This emphasises that since assessments have a practical purpose they should be based on a practical knowledge of the condition and of its manifestations, treatability and prognosis.

Many patients can be perfectly adequately assessed by general practitioners. Indeed, a close, long term acquaintance between the doctor and the patient may be a major asset in enhancing the patient's capacity. However, it is important to emphasise that a general practitioner's close and personal knowledge of a patient, even concern and affection, must not be allowed to interfere with an objective assessment about the patient's actual mental disabilities and implied (in)capacities. Sometimes it will be appropriate for a general practitioner and a hospital specialist to consult together in determining their individual views of the patient's capacity. This offers the advantage of combining expertise in the management of a complicated condition with close acquaintance with the patient. Examples of relevant specialist opinions, in relation to particular diagnoses might be as follows:

- Consultant general psychiatrist: schizophrenia, severe depressive illness, hypomania, paranoid psychosis;
- Consultant psycho-geriatrician: Alzheimer's Disease or other dementias;
- Consultant psychiatrist in learning disability: learning disability or mental handicap;

- Consultant neurologist or consultant neuropsychiatrist: head injury;
- Consultant general psychiatrist or consultant general psychiatrist with a special interest in eating disorders: anorexia nervosa;
- Consultant neurologist or consultant neurosurgeon: brain tumour.

13:2.2 Other disciplines

Any medical opinion should take full account of relevant information from other disciplines. An assessment by a clinical psychologist may already be available, or could be sought, and this may assist in giving a detailed, validated and systematic assessment of cognitive functioning. An occupational therapist might properly be consulted when information about daily functioning is of importance. Again, a report from a nurse or from an approved social worker may sometimes be helpful where information about daily functioning or social functioning is of importance. This again emphasises that it is not a diagnosis *per se* which is important but specific disabilities.

13:2.3 Medico-legal expertise

In a complex medico-legal case it may be important for a lawyer to choose a doctor with particular experience in medico-legal work. Experience of sifting through large volumes of medical and other information and experience of some of the potential complexities of the interface between medicine and law can greatly assist a clear presentation of the medical issues. However, it is important that experts are chosen primarily for their medical knowledge and not because they "do a lot of court work". Medical knowledge plus medico-legal experience is often a helpful combination.

13:3 Psychiatric diagnoses

13:3.1 Categories of diagnoses

A psychiatric diagnosis may be attributable to any condition which primarily presents with mental symptoms and signs. Psychiatric diagnoses are initially conveniently subdivided into (a) organic and (b) functional.

(a) *Organic conditions* can arise from brain disorders or from some general malfunction of the body (for example, of the endocrine or hormone system). Brain disorders can be further subdivided into acute (for example, an acute confusional state from urinary retention or from a toxic infective cause) and chronic (for example, dementia), the latter also being distinguished into congenital (for example, learning disability) or acquired (for example, from a head injury).

(b) *Functional disorders* are divided into mental illness (which involves a change in the person's mental state away from their usual, normal state and which can either be temporary or permanent) and personality disorder (which is a developmental disorder, inherent, and essentially permanent). Mental illnesses can be divided into "psychotic" and "neurotic". Psychotic illnesses (for example, schizophrenia, hypomania, psychotic depression) involve lack of insight and the experience of delusions and hallucinations (not arising from organic causes). Neurotic illnesses (for example, mild to moderate depression, anxiety disorders, obsessive-compulsive disorders) include insight and often a request for treatment. A very few conditions sit on the "border" between psychotic and neurotic. Hence, anorexia nervosa presents with a particular mix of features where there are no hallucinations and strictly no delusions but where there is substantial distortion of body perception and profoundly distorted forms of cognition.

One can think of diagnostic categories as existing in a hierarchy. Hence:

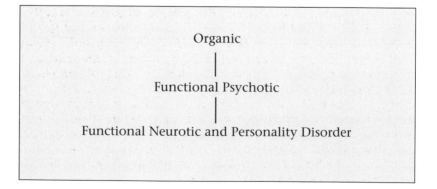

It is important to note that a patient can satisfy the diagnostic criteria for more than one diagnosis. This is diagnostically acceptable but, in terms of capacity, it is likely that the features of the higher order diagnosis will be of greater significance.

13:3.2 Specific diagnoses

Aside from broad diagnostic categories, specific psychiatric diagnoses are made on the basis of particular clusters of symptoms and signs. Although there is a tendency for these clusters to overlap somewhat (and this can give rise to diagnostic disputes), proper concentration on specific symptoms and signs will mean that this overlap is usually relatively unimportant. The broad categorical classification system just given may be of more use in suggesting capacity, or its absence, than a specific diagnosis (particularly bearing in mind the importance of attention to specific symptoms and signs in any event).

There are two accepted international systems for the classification of mental disorders. It is helpful if medical reports tie the diagnosis into one of these systems to ensure diagnostic reliability (between doctors). This is further explained in section 12:4.

13:4 Medical assessment of mental conditions

Although capacity may be influenced by physical conditions it is crucially important for any assessing doctor to take a full psychiatric history and to carry out a mental state examination, as well as a general medical assessment of the person. In psychiatry "symptoms" are what the patient tells you and "signs" are the doctor's objective observation of the patient. However, in psychiatric assessment, although some signs are clearly objective (a depressed patient may be dishevelled when usually kempt) many signs involve a medical interpretation of the patient's symptom complaints (for example: does a patient's complaint about "voices" really amount to auditory hallucinations; is a strange belief held with such conviction that it amounts to a delusion?). This can introduce a degree of ambiguity which is less common in other branches of medicine. However, it is not the case that psychiatric assessments are inherently personal to the individual doctor or inherently ambiguous. High levels of diagnostic reliability should be expected.

Psychiatric assessment includes assessment for both organic and functional conditions. Hence, assessment should always include at least a brief physical assessment and, when indicated by the history or by physical observation, more detailed physical examination and investigation. The following describes briefly the process of psychiatric assessment.

13:4.1 History

History of presenting complaint — This is a description by the patient of his or her main complaints (symptoms). The doctor will pursue symptoms, through asking specific direct questions aimed at elucidating the symptoms and specifically considering possible differential diagnoses. When it is known that the assessment is in relation to "capacity" it may also be appropriate to pursue certain relevant symptoms in detail and to ask questions specifically relevant to the particular capacity concerned.

Background history — This includes a brief description of the patient's personal history, family history, psychosexual history (including obstetric and gynaecological history), social history and previous forensic history.

Pre-morbid personality — This is a description by the patient (or sometimes more appropriately by a relative or others) of the patient's usual personality (that is, when not mentally or otherwise ill). This is important as a baseline against which the patient's current symptom complaints (and presentation at interview) can be set.

Previous medical history — This will detail all non-psychiatric conditions and treatments, including reference to any drugs that the patient is currently taking. The history may give clues as to a physical cause of apparently psychiatric symptoms.

Previous psychiatric history — This can be of relevance to current mental state assessment. A history of previous disorder may give clues about the origins of present symptoms (or signs).

Drugs and alcohol history — This may be of great relevance to the determination of the differential diagnosis of mental disorder (since drugs or chronic alcohol abuse can cause psychiatric presentations).

Information from others — This is important because patients may misrepresent symptoms (either hiding them or exaggerating them) or they may describe their usual personality in a way which is heavily influenced by their current illness (for example, depressed patients may describe themselves as being "useless" and "incapable at work" whereas the reverse is the case). Of course, in assessing a person for some legal capacity the person providing the information may be someone who has a vested interest (either social or financial) in the doctor's assessment of the patient's capacity and care must be taken to allow for this possibility. Information from a number of people may assist in sifting out truth from bias.

13:4.2 Mental state examination

This is an objective assessment of the patient's mental functioning. The purpose of such an examination is to define specific abnormalities (and disabilities) and to establish a diagnosis. It is only through detailed assessment of specific aspects of mental functioning that capacity can properly be assessed. The following features will be relevant in any assessment carried out by a doctor:

- appearance and behaviour
- speech
- mood
- thought
- perception
- cognition
- memory
- intelligence
- orientation
- insight

A full explanation of the process of the mental state examination is set out in section 12:5.

13:4.3 Physical examination

Psychiatric assessment may properly include a brief physical assessment. In some cases, where indicated by the history or by physical observation, a more detailed physical examination and investigation may be required. It is important to keep in mind that an apparent psychiatric presentation can be reflective of an organic neurological disorder and some patients can present neurologically and yet have a primary psychiatric condition (hysterical symptoms being an obvious example). Central (brain) neurology and psychiatry are often intricately intertwined. Indeed, conditions such as dementia are, in a sense, both "psychiatric" and "neurological". Again, some recognised "psychiatric" conditions, such as schizophrenia, have demonstrable organic aspects and are also probably partially determined by genetic predisposition perhaps expressed through brain abnormality.

13:4.4 Case notes

It is important for the assessing doctors to have access to all relevant medical and psychiatric records. These will give an historical picture of a known current disorder, as well as giving diagnostic clues to a so far undiagnosed current disorder. In assessing capacity an historical view may be of particular importance, especially in relation both to the likely response to treatment and to prognosis, since these may affect future capacity. Indeed, assessment of the permanence or transience of disabilities may be crucially important in offering a view about capacity (especially where the legal process can be delayed).

13:5 Conclusion

Accurate assessment of capacity depends upon clarity on the part of both lawyers and doctors about the relationship between legal and medical concepts. It therefore depends upon doctors knowing something about the law and lawyers understanding something of medical assessment and diagnosis. This chapter and the preceding one should therefore be read as two sides of a single coin.

Appendix A

DRAFT

OF A

BILL

TO

Make new provision in relation to mentally incapacitated A.D. 1995. persons; to confer new functions on local authorities in relation to persons in need of care or protection; and for connected purposes.

BE IT ENACTED by the Queen's most Excellent Majesty, by and with the advice and consent of the Lords Spiritual and Temporal, and Commons, in this present Parliament assembled, and by the authority of the same, as follows:-

PART I
MENTAL INCAPACITY

CHAPTER I
PRELIMINARY

1.— (1) This Part of this Act has effect — Purpose of
Part I.

    (a) for conferring statutory authority, subject to specified restrictions, for things done for the personal welfare or health care of a person without capacity; and

    (b) for enabling decisions to be made on behalf of such a person by the donee of a power of attorney (in this Act referred to as a "continuing power of attorney") which complies with the requirements of this Part of this Act, by the court or by a manager appointed by the court.

    (2) Except as otherwise provided, this Part of this Act does not enable anything to be done for, or a decision to be made on behalf of, a person who has not attained the age of sixteen.

2.— (1) For the purposes of this Part of this Act a person is Persons
without capacity if at the material time — without
capacity.

(a) he is unable by reason of mental disability to make a decision for himself on the matter in question; or

(b) he is unable to communicate his decision on that matter because he is unconscious or for any other reason.

(2) For the purposes of this Part of this Act a person is at the material time unable to make a decision by reason of mental disability if the disability is such that at the time when the decision needs to be made —

(a) he is unable to understand or retain the information relevant to the decision, including information about the reasonably foreseeable consequences of deciding one way or another or of failing to make the decision; or

(b) he is unable to make a decision based on that information,

and in this Act "mental disability" means a disability or disorder of the mind or brain, whether permanent or temporary, which results in an impairment or disturbance of mental functioning.

(3) A person shall not be regarded as unable to understand the information referred to in subsection (2)(a) above if he is able to understand an explanation of that information in broad terms and in simple language.

(4) A person shall not be regarded as unable to make a decision by reason of mental disability merely because he makes a decision which would not be made by a person of ordinary prudence.

(5) A person shall not be regarded as unable to communicate his decision unless all practicable steps to enable him to do so have been taken without success.

(6) There shall be a presumption against lack of capacity and any question whether a person lacks capacity shall be decided on the balance of probabilities.

3.— (1) Anything done for, and any decision made on behalf of, a person by virtue of this Part of this Act shall be done or made in his best interests.

(2) In deciding what is in a person's best interests regard shall be had to the following —

(a) so far as ascertainable, his past and present wishes and feelings and the factors which he would consider if he were able to do so;

(b) the need to permit and encourage that person to participate, or to improve his ability to participate, as fully as possible in anything done for and any decision affecting him;

(c) if it is practicable and appropriate to consult them, the views as to that person's wishes and feelings and as to what would be in his best interests of —

(i) any person named by him as someone to be consulted on those matters;

(ii) anyone (whether his spouse, a relative, friend or other person) engaged in caring for him or interested in his welfare;

(iii) the donee of any continuing power of attorney granted by him;

(iv) any manager appointed for him by the court;

(d) whether the purpose for which any action or decision is required can be as effectively achieved in a manner less restrictive of his freedom of action.

PART I
CHAPTER I

(3) In the case of anything done or a decision made by a person other than the court it shall be a sufficient compliance with subsection (1) above if that person reasonably believes that what he does or decides is in the best interests of the person concerned.

CHAPTER II

CARE OF PERSON WITHOUT CAPACITY

General authority

4.— (1) Subject to the provisions of this Chapter, it shall be lawful to do anything for the personal welfare or health care of a person who is, or is reasonably believed to be, without capacity in relation to the matter in question ("the person concerned") if it is in all the circumstances reasonable for it to be done by the person who does it.

Power to provide care.

(2) Where what is done by virtue of this section involves expenditure it shall be lawful —

    (a) for that purpose to pledge the credit of the person concerned; and

    (b) to apply money in the possession of the person concerned for meeting the expenditure;

and if the expenditure is borne for him by another person that person shall be entitled to reimburse himself out of any such money or to be otherwise indemnified by the person concerned.

(3) Subsection (2) above is without prejudice to any power to spend money for the benefit of the person concerned which is exercisable apart from this section by virtue of having lawful control of money or other property of his.

(4) Schedule 1 to this Act shall have effect for enabling certain payments which would otherwise be made to a person without capacity to be made instead to a person acting on his behalf or to be otherwise dealt with as provided in that Schedule.

Restrictions on general authority

5.— (1) Subject to subsection (2) below, section 4 above does not authorise — No powers of coercion.

    (a) the use or threat of force to enforce the doing of anything to which the person concerned objects; or

    (b) the detention or confinement of that person whether or not he objects.

(2) This section does not preclude the taking of any steps necessary to avert a substantial risk of serious harm to the person concerned.

Appendix B

Case Studies

Case 1

Archie is 81 and was formerly a high-ranking civil servant. He now suffers from senile dementia manifested primarily by a short term memory deficit. Four years ago he had two small strokes which have contributed to the onset of his memory deficit. His wife, Barbara, died last year and since her death he has only been able to remain in his own home with the support of a neighbour, Connie, whom he often refers to as Barbara. His next of kin is a son who lives 200 miles away and rarely visits him. Archie has an estate worth roughly £350,000. The value of his house is about £125,000 and, although he has no mortgage, he has the usual outgoings to pay – Council Tax, water charges, gas, electricity, telephone and insurance – and there are his normal day-to-day living expenses. He has £75,000 in banks and building societies, and a portfolio of shares and unit trusts worth approximately £150,000. The income from his occupational pension, state pension and investments comes to about £17,000 a year.

Archie recently wrote to his solicitor saying that he wanted to make a new will leaving a legacy of £50,000 to Connie. He also hinted that he was thinking about marrying her. With Archie's consent the solicitor contacted his GP, explained the situation and mentioned that it would probably be necessary to carry out at least four separate assessments of capacity (spread over several visits). Archie also agreed that any confidential information about his property and affairs which might be relevant could be disclosed to his GP. The specific tests the solicitor had in mind were for:

(a) capacity to create an enduring power of attorney (EPA);

(b) capacity to manage and administer his property and affairs;

(c) capacity to make a will; and

(d) capacity to marry.

On her first visit, the GP established that Archie was capable of creating an enduring power of attorney appointing the solicitor as attorney. Archie was capable of understanding and did understand that:

- the attorney would be able to assume complete authority over his affairs;
- the attorney would in general be able to do anything with his property that he could have done personally;
- the authority given under the enduring power would continue if he should be or become mentally incapable; and
- if he should be or become mentally incapable, he could not revoke the enduring power of attorney without confirmation by the Court of Protection.

However, the GP was also of the opinion that Archie was "incapable, by reason of mental disorder, of managing and administering his property and affairs". This involved establishing first that he has a "mental disorder" as defined in the Mental Health Act 1983. There was no problem here. Archie suffers from dementia, a mental illness characterised by "more than temporary impairment of intellectual functions shown by a failure of memory, orientation, comprehension and learning capacity" (see section 3:2.2). Secondly, it had to be established that, by reason of his mental disorder, he was or was becoming incapable of managing and administering his property and affairs.

Archie then made an EPA appointing the solicitor as his attorney. The GP witnessed Archie's execution of the power. Before executing the power the solicitor warned Archie that because the GP was of the opinion that he was incapable by reason of mental disorder of managing and administering his property and affairs, the solicitor, as attorney, would be under a duty to register the EPA with the Court of Protection straightaway. If Archie had not made, or had been incapable of making, an enduring power, someone could have applied to the Court of Protection for a person to be appointed as his receiver (see section 3:2).

Connie has been a great support to him during the last 12 months. Without her assistance - doing the shopping, cooking, cleaning, laundry and ironing, as well as occasional help washing and dressing him when he has a bad day - it would have been impossible for him to have remained in his own home for as long as he has. However, his finances are potentially vulnerable. We hear a lot about elder abuse these days, but this phenomenon is not just physical, psychological or sexual. Financial exploitation is probably the most prevalent form of elder abuse.

Archie has already bought Connie a new Ford Escort. Admittedly, he is the principal beneficiary because she spends most of her time driving him around in it. Although it cost about £11,000, the validity of the gift is not in doubt. It was intended to be an outright gift - a token of his appreciation - and its value is insignificant in the context of his assets as a whole (see chapter 5). He hasn't driven it himself yet, although, in theory, he could if he wanted to. He still has a valid driving licence. From the age of 70 drivers have to re-apply for a licence every three years. When he completed the renewal application two years ago, he did not consider that he was suffering from any kind of mental disorder that might affect his ability to drive. The GP tells the solicitor that she considers that it would be unsafe for Archie to drive. Archie's solicitor informs him that he must report his illness to the Driver and Vehicle Licensing Agency who may revoke his licence. Archie agrees.

Having resolved the questions of Archie's capacity to create an enduring power of attorney and manage and administer his property and affairs, the solicitor then had to deal with his ability to make a will, otherwise known as "testamentary capacity". The solicitor explained to the GP that Archie should:

(i)   understand the nature and effect of making a will;
(ii) understand the effect of the will he proposes to make;
(iii) understand the extent (rather than the actual value) of the property of which he is disposing under the will; and
(iv) comprehend and appreciate the claims to which he ought to give effect.

The first three points are based on "understanding". This entails receiving, evaluating and reaching a decision on information either known to him already, or communicated and explained to him in broad terms and simple language by a third party, perhaps the solicitor. The final stage encompasses more than understanding - it involves Archie's judgment. He must be capable of weighing the respective merits of Connie, whom he sees every day and who has been of sterling assistance to him during the last 12 months, and his son, whom he rarely sees, but who is nevertheless his next of kin. This is far harder to assess because it is extremely subjective. There is also a danger that the assessor might consider Archie's decision to be foolish, but it is his capacity - rather than his wisdom - that is being assessed. Furthermore, being able to comprehend and appreciate the claims to which he ought to give effect is something that Archie must be capable of doing without help from anyone else.

The GP had to admit that she found it impossible to decide whether Archie had testamentary capacity. The solicitor then contacted a clinical psychologist who had assessed Archie's memory problems a couple of years ago. The clinical psychologist spent an hour and a half assessing his testamentary capacity, and was able to readminister a couple of the tests applied in the earlier assessment (the Modified Mini-Mental State Examination, and the Wechsler Memory Scale). He concluded that, on the balance of probabilities, Archie had testamentary capacity, despite his short term memory deficit. Accordingly, a will was prepared in accordance with the instructions originally contained in the letter to the solicitor, which Archie had subsequently confirmed in his conversations with those assessing his testamentary capacity. The GP and the clinical psychologist were asked to act as witnesses when Archie signed the will because of the so-called "golden if tactless rule" that "when a solicitor is drawing up a will for an aged testator or one who has been seriously ill, it should be witnessed or approved by a medical practitioner, who ought to record his examination of the testator and his findings" (see section 4:3).

If it had been decided that, on the balance of probabilities, Archie lacked testamentary capacity, the solicitor would have considered applying to the Court of Protection for an order under the Mental Health Act 1983 authorising the execution of a statutory will on his behalf (see section 4:6). Because such an application would have been made on behalf of the donor of a registered enduring power of attorney, the Court would have required medical evidence of both (a) his testamentary capacity, and (b) his capacity to manage and administer his property and affairs. If it had been necessary to apply for a statutory will, Archie's son would have been given notice of the application by the Court. But because Archie was capable of making a valid will for himself, the solicitor had no obligation to inform the son about the changes his father proposed to make to his will. Indeed, to have told the son would have constituted a breach of the solicitor's duty to keep a client's affairs confidential until the client permits disclosure or waives the confidentiality (see section 1:4.1).

The final type of capacity to be assessed was whether Archie is capable of entering into a valid marriage (see section 9:2). There is an additional complication here. A will is automatically revoked when the person who made it gets married, unless the will was specifically expressed to be made in expectation of that marriage. Archie and Connie are not engaged yet and, at the moment, have no definite plans to marry. The will was not, therefore, expressed to be made in expectation of their forthcoming marriage. If he does eventually marry her, a further assessment of Archie's testamentary capacity will be necessary. If it is concluded that he lacks testamentary capacity at that time, an application could be made to the Court of Protection for the execution of a statutory will. If he still has testamentary capacity he could, of course, make a valid will for himself.

It has been suggested that the capacity required to enter into a valid marriage is relatively low. If Archie and Connie decide to get married, it will be necessary to establish whether he is capable of giving valid consent (and that, for instance, she is not pressurising him into marrying her against his will), and that he understands the nature of marriage and respective rights and responsibilities of husband and wife. Their friendship has allegedly assumed a sexual dimension, but his capacity to consent to sexual relations is not an issue (see section 9:3).

Case 2

John is in his late sixties and has been diagnosed as suffering from chronic schizophrenia. He has delusions that people are interfering with his thoughts and that they are also trying to harm him. John has developed an acute infection of a limb which is life threatening. It is explained to him that if he does not have the limb removed there is a high probability that he will die. John refuses consent to the surgery but says he will accept the alternative of antibiotics, even intravenously. It is unlikely that this will substantially reduce the risk of death, certainly in the medium term and perhaps even immediately. What are the possible medico-legal implications of this clinical situation?

Nothing would be gained by detaining John under the Mental Health Act 1983. The Act allows, in certain circumstances, non-consensual treatment but only for mental disorders or their consequences. John suffers from a physical condition which is unrelated to his mental state and psychiatric diagnosis. Hence, only common law provisions are relevant.

A diagnosis of schizophrenia does not automatically imply a lack of capacity to consent to or refuse consent to treatment at common law. What matters is the nature of a person's mental state abnormalities and how they relate to the definition in law of capacity, that is, "the capacity to understand in broad terms the nature and purpose of the proposed treatment". Only if a patient lacks capacity according to this definition can the common law be invoked so as to treat the patient without consent (see chapter 10).

Much more would need to be known about John's psychiatric symptoms than have been described so far before a conclusion as to the patient's capacity could be reached. If, for example, he had incorporated the treatment information and/or treatment personnel into his paranoid delusions then, although this may not interfere with his capacity to "receive and retain" the treatment information (and information about the consequences of non-treatment), it may well inhibit or impair his capacity to "believe" what he is being told or to "weigh" that information in coming to a decision. However, if the delusions were unconnected with the treatment information and the medical personnel, and therefore unconnected with his decision about surgical treatment, John would have capacity to refuse consent.

If, however, John later became septicemic (from the local infection) then, at that point, any cognitive abnormality arising from an acute confusional state might well result in a lack of capacity. He could then be treated under the doctrine of necessity (see section 10:4.3.1). However, had John (a) previously obtained a court declaration that he had capacity to refuse the treatment and that the procedure should not be carried out without his consent, and (b) made an "advance directive" (see section 10:6.2) that he could not be treated without his consent in the future, then even the supervening acute confusional state (and lack of capacity) would fail to render lawful surgical intervention (so long as it was for the same physical condition). John could, of course, revoke the effect of the advance directive in the future so long as he had the capacity to do so.

If, having so far survived his local infection, John subsequently had a stroke, then specific cognitive abnormalities might interfere with his capacity to receive and/or retain treatment information, as well as, depending upon the area of the brain affected by the stroke, his capacity to weigh that information. It might, alternatively, give rise to a disability limited to verbal expression (for example, nominal aphasia). If so, every effort should be made to limit the impact of John's communication difficulties rather than to equate it with incapacity. In the event that capacity was significantly impaired and John had already made an advance directive whilst competent, the directive would be effective notwithstanding the supervening incapacity. John's earlier refusal could not be overridden and he would have lost the capacity to revoke the original advance directive. If, however, a different physical condition arose which was not covered by the advance directive, then the doctrine of necessity could justify treatment for that condition without consent (if John now lacked capacity). Indeed any treatment of the stroke itself could be carried out under the same principle.

Case 3

Jane is 19 years old and has Down's Syndrome. When she was 11 years old her mother died and Jane was placed by her father in residential care. She lived with several foster families for short periods but was finally permanently placed at the age of 13 with a family. For part of this time and until she was 18 Jane lived with the family under the provisions of a Residence Order obtained as a result of proceedings brought under the Children Act 1989. During this period Jane continued to see her father during occasional weekends and had contact with him through letters and telephone calls.

When Jane became 18 she was entitled to decide where she wished to live. She was very clear that she wished to continue to live with her present family which is a large "extended family". Soon after her eighteenth birthday Jane became engaged to marry and subsequently married someone she met on her college course. He also has Down's Syndrome and they both live in independent accommodation within the "extended family".

Before her marriage Jane's father asked to her to return to live with him and his second wife. Jane had not lived with her father since she was 11 and stated clearly that she did not wish to return to live with her father but wished to continue to live with her present "family". This decision caused conflict between Jane's father and her current carers/family. Jane became very upset and distressed by this and by her father's continued contact which she said was unpleasant. She stated that she did not wish to see her father at all or have any cards or letters from him. Subsequent to this Jane married her husband and they both remain living at her home and have no contact with her father but have contact which is positive and supportive from her husband's family.

Jane's father has now started proceedings in the Family Division of the High Court to ask the Court to make a declaration as to where Jane should live and that it would be in her best interests to have contact with him. Jane continues to say that she does not wish to have contact with her father or his family and that she wishes to continue to live where she is.

Jane subsequently instructed her own solicitor. The solicitor met with Jane on a number of occasions both in her own home and in the solicitor's office and came to the decision that Jane understood that she wished to continue to live in her present home and that she understood that the solicitor would be speaking for her when the solicitor wrote to Jane's father's solicitors. Jane also has an advocate who meets with Jane and her solicitor to assist Jane in representing her views to the solicitor.

Despite attempts at negotiation through the solicitors the Court proceedings continue. Jane's father is seeking a declaration to force Jane either to live with him and/or have contact with him. Jane maintains that she does not wish to live with her father or to see him. Although Jane has Down's Syndrome she has good language ability. The first stage of the proceedings involves consideration by the Court as to whether Jane has capacity to instruct her solicitor. If the Court decides on the basis of expert reports that Jane does not have capacity to manage and administer her property and affairs and therefore instruct her solicitor then the Court will consider whether it has jurisdiction to make a declaration about what is in her best interests.

The present issue is whether Jane does understand enough to instruct her solicitor on the question of who she should see and where she should live. The solicitor has taken the view that on this particular issue Jane has capacity and can instruct the solicitor. There are other issues in Jane's life which are now being considered in relation to capacity. Her father is now considering challenging her marriage on the grounds that she had no capacity to consent to the marriage. There is also concern about Jane's ability to manage her money and affairs and whether someone should be appointed to do this for her.

Each of the decisions which Jane has to make must be decided with a different test of capacity. Medical evidence which has been sought is at present conflicting and it may be necessary to present more detailed evidence about Jane's day-to-day understanding of her world, in particular her ability to function on a range of tasks and skills. Jane is a vulnerable person and is susceptible to influence by others. It is very important to make sure that her decisions are as far as possible made voluntarily by her. It is, of course, very difficult for any person to make a decision which is independent of the views of others with whom the person lives or has relationships. This case presents dilemmas of ensuring a high quality of care and protection for an individual who is vulnerable and who has impaired capacity in specific tasks but who wishes to maintain her independence and decision-making capacity to the maximum extent possible.

Case 4

Michael is 29 years old and suffers from severe brain damage sustained in a road accident when he was 18 years old. Until the age of 18 he lived with his mother, step-father, brother and step-sister. He left school at 16 and became a trainee chef and was successful in his career. Immediately after the accident Michael was cared for in an acute neurological ward where he was severely ill and for much of the time in a coma. He gradually recovered consciousness and was transferred to a rehabilitation hospital where planning for his future care began.

Michael's parents had divorced when Michael was 10 and his mother had obtained custody of Michael and his brother. The divorce had been acrimonious. Michael had seen his father between the ages of 11 and 19 very rarely. His father had moved away and maintained only occasional contact with his two sons.

When Michael was receiving treatment at the rehabilitation hospital all his family including his father and step-mother visited. There were clinical meetings to discuss Michael's discharge and it was always planned that he would return home to live with his mother and step-father. That way he could continue to have contact with old friends. While Michael was in hospital there was much conflict between his mother and father and subsequently Michael's father came to the hospital and removed him, taking him home to live with him and his second wife.

Michael's mother consulted a solicitor and was informed that there was nothing she could do and that she should try to sort this out with Michael's father. Michael's father refused to talk about Michael's future and certainly did not wish Michael to return home to live with his mother. His father maintained that this was what Michael would have wanted and Michael continued to live with his father and step-mother and attend a day centre for head injured patients near their home. Believing that there was nothing further she could do Michael's mother lost contact with him.

Now, on the advice of another solicitor, Michael's mother has commenced proceedings in the High Court to ask the Court to make a declaration as to Michael's best interests with regard to increasing contact with her and the rest of his family and as to where he should live in the future.

At present the day-to-day care of Michael currently rests with his father and step-mother and they make most of his day-to-day decisions. Michael is unable to initiate contact with his mother by telephone, by letter or by actively going to see her. The current issue is whether Michael is able to make the decision about whether he wishes to see his mother. His father maintains that Michael does not wish to have contact with his family and that Michael is able to make this decision.

After Michael's accident solicitors acting on his behalf instituted a damages claim and a large award of damages was subsequently made. His affairs are managed by the Court of Protection and the Public Trustee has been appointed as his receiver by the Court of Protection to manage his affairs (see section 3:2). Despite this Michael may be able to make his own decisions about other matters including whether to see his mother and whether he wishes to live with his mother or his father. Medical experts are being sought to assess Michael's degree of brain damage and psychological evidence is being sought to assess his understanding of his world and where he lives. Any decision about Michael's capacity would be based on specific situations about which he is asked to make decisions. There is a legal structure to enable others to make financial decisions on his behalf but no legal structure to enable others to make personal decisions on his behalf. Michael's life is currently affected by those around him and in particular by his father and step-mother who live with him on a day-to-day basis and at the moment control much of his personal life.

Appendix C

Useful Addresses

The British Medical Association

BMA House
Tavistock Square
London WC1H 9JP
Tel: 0171 387 4499

Medical Ethics:
Tel: 0171 383 6286

The Law Society

113 Chancery Lane
London WC2A 1PL
DX 56 London/Chancery Lane
Tel: 0171 242 1222

*Mental Health and Disability
Committee* Tel: 0171 320 5695

Practice Advice Service:
Tel: 0171 320 5338/5339

Professional Ethics Division
Ipsley Court
Berrington Close
Redditch
Worcs B98 0TD
DX 19114 Redditch
Tel: 0171 242 1222
(local calls: 01527 51741)

Official Addresses

Court of Protection

Stewart House
24 Kingsway
London WC2B 6JX
DX 37965 London/Kingsway
Tel: 0171 269 7157

Principal Registry of the Family Division

Somerset House
Strand
London WC2R 1LP
DX 396 London/Chancery Lane
Tel: 0171 936 6000

The Official Solicitor of the Supreme Court

81 Chancery Lane
London WC2A 1DD
DX 0012 London/Chancery Lane
Tel: 0171 911 7127

Public Trust Office Agency

Stewart House
24 Kingsway
London WC2B 6JX
DX 37965 London/Kingsway
Tel: 0171 269 7300

Royal Courts of Justice

Strand
London WC1A 2LL
DX 44450 London/Strand
Tel: 0171 936 6000

Treasury Solicitor

28 Broadway
London SW1H 9JX
DX 2318 London/Victoria 1
Tel: 0171 210 3000

Social Services Inspectorate

Wellington House
133-155 Waterloo Road
London SE1 8UG
Tel: 0171 972 2000

General

Action on Elder Abuse

Astral House
1268 London Road
London SW16 4ER
Tel: 0181 679 2648

Age Concern England

Astral House
1268 London Road
London SW16 4ER
Tel: 0181 679 8000

Carers National Association

2025 Glasshouse Yard
London EC1A 1JS
Tel: 0171 490 8898

Down's Syndrome Association

153-5 Mitcham Road
London SW17 9PG
Tel: 0181 682 4001

Age Concern Cymru

4th Floor
1 Cathedral Road
Cardiff CF1 9SD
Tel: 01222 371566

Alzheimer's Disease Society

Gordon House
10 Greencoat Place
London SW1P 1PH
Tel: 0171 306 0606

Counsel and Care for the Elderly

Twyman House
16 Bonny Street
London NW1 9PG
Tel: 0171 485 1566

Help the Aged

16-18 St James's Walk
London EC1R OBE
Tel: 0171 253 0253

MIND
*(National Association for
Mental Health)*

Granta House
15-19 Broadway
London E15 4BQ
Tel: 0181 519 2122

National Autistic Society

276 Willesden Lane
London NW2 5RB
Tel: 0171 637 0741

SANE

199 Old Marylebone Road
London NW1 5QP
Tel: 0171 724 8000

Mencap
*(Royal Society for Mentally
Handicapped Children and Adults)*

123 Golden Lane
London EC1Y ORT
Tel: 0171 454 0454

Patients Association

8 Gilford Street
London WC1N 1DT
Tel: 0171 242 3460

Appendix D

PRACTICE NOTE

(OFFICIAL SOLICITOR: STERILISATION)

1 The sterilisation of a minor or a mentally incompetent adult ("the Patient") will in virtually all cases require the prior sanction of a High Court Judge: Re B (A Minor) (Wardship: Sterilisation) [1988] AC 199; Re F [1990] 2 AC 1; Re HG (Specific Issue Order: Sterilisation) [1993] 1 FLR 587.

2 Applications in respect of a minor should be made in the Family Division of the High Court, within proceedings either under the inherent jurisdiction or Section 8(1) ("a specific issue order") of the Children Act 1989. In the Official Solicitor's view, the procedural and administrative difficulties attaching to applications under Section 8 of the Children Act 1989 are such that the preferred course is to apply within the inherent jurisdiction.

Within the inherent jurisdiction, applicants should seek an order in the following or a broadly similar form:

"It is ordered that there be leave to perform an operation of sterilisation on the minor [X] [*if it is desired to specify the precise method of carrying out the operation add, eg, by the occlusion of her fallopian tubes*] and to carry out such post-operative treatment and care as may be necessary in her best interests."

Within proceedings under section 8 of the Children Act 1989, applicants should seek an order in the following or a broadly similar form:

"THE COURT ORDERS, in determining the specific question which has arisen in connection with the exercise of parental responsibility by [A & B] in respect of the minor [X] as to whether it is in the minor's best interests to perform an operation of sterilisation on her [*if it is desired to specify the precise method of carrying out the operation add, eg, by the occlusion of her fallopian tubes*], THAT such an operation is in her best

interests and can lawfully be performed on her [*AND that [A &
B] can give a valid consent thereto*]."

3 Applications in respect of an adult should be by way of
Originating Summons issuing out of the Family Division of the
High Court for an order in the following or a broadly similar
form:

"It is declared that the operation of sterilisation proposed to be
performed on [X] [*if it is desired to specify the precise method
of carrying out the operation, add eg, by the occlusion of her fallopian tubes*] being in the existing circumstances in her best
interests can lawfully be performed on her despite her inability
to consent to it.

It is ordered that in the event of a material change in the
existing circumstances occurring before the said operation has
been performed any party shall have liberty to apply for such
further or other declaration or order as may be just."

4 The Plaintiff or Applicant should normally be a parent or one
of those responsible for the care of the Patient or those intend-
ing to carry out the proposed operation. The Patient must
always be a party and should normally be a Defendant or
Respondent. In cases in which the Patient is a Defendant or
Respondent the Patient's Guardian ad litem should normally
be the Official Solicitor. In any case in which the Official
Solicitor is not either the Next Friend or the Guardian ad litem
of the Patient or a Plaintiff or Applicant he shall be a
Defendant or Respondent.

5 Prior to the substantive hearing of the application there will in
every case be a summons for directions which will be heard by
a High Court Judge. The Principal Registry will fix a date for
directions before a Judge of the Family Division on the first
open date after the passage of eight weeks when asked to do so
at the issue of the Originating Summons.

6 The purpose of the proceedings is to establish whether or not
the proposed sterilisation is in the best interests of the Patient.
The Judge will require to be satisfied that those proposing
sterilisation are seeking it in good faith and that their
paramount concern is for the best interests of the Patient rather

than their own or the public's convenience. The proceedings will normally involve a thorough adversarial investigation of all possible viewpoints and any possible alternatives to sterilisation. Nevertheless, straightforward cases proceeding without dissent may be disposed of at the hearing for directions without oral evidence.

7 The Official Solicitor will act as either an independent and disinterested guardian representing the interests of the Patient, or as an ex officio defendant. In whichever capacity he acts, he will carry out his own investigations, call his own witnesses and take whatever other steps appear to him to be necessary in order to ensure that all relevant matters are thoroughly aired before the Judge, including cross-examining the expert and other witnesses called in support of the proposed operation and presenting all reasonable arguments against sterilisation. The Official Solicitor will require to meet and interview the Patient in private in all cases where he or she is able to express any views (however limited) about the legal proceedings, the prospect of sterilisation, parenthood, other means of contraception or other relevant matters.

8 The Official Solicitor anticipates that the Judge will expect to receive comprehensive medical, psychological and social evaluations of the Patient from appropriately qualified experts. Without in any way attempting either to define or to limit the factors which may require to be taken into account in any particular case the Official Solicitor anticipates that the Judge will normally require evidence clearly establishing:

(1) That (a) the patient is incapable of making his or her own decision about sterilisation and (b) the Patient is unlikely to develop sufficiently to make an informed judgement about sterilisation in the foreseeable future. (In this connection it must be borne in mind (i) that the fact that a person is legally incompetent for some purposes does not mean that he or she necessarily lacks the capacity to make a decision about sterilisation and (ii) that in the case of a minor his or her youth and potential for development may make it difficult or impossible to make the relevant finding of incapacity.)

(2) That the condition which it is sought to avoid will in fact occur, eg, in the case of a contraceptive sterilisation that there is a need for contraception because (a) the Patient is physically capable of procreation and (b) the Patient is likely to engage in sexual activity, at the present or in the near future, under circumstances where there is a real danger as opposed to mere chance that pregnancy is likely to result.

(3) That the Patient will experience substantial trauma or psychological damage if the condition which it is sought to avoid should arise, eg, in the case of a contraceptive sterilisation that (a) the Patient (if a woman) is likely if she becomes pregnant or gives birth to experience substantial trauma or psychological damage greater than that resulting from the sterilisation itself and (b) the Patient is permanently incapable of caring for a child even with reasonable assistance, eg, from a future spouse in a case where the Patient has or may have the capacity to marry.

(4) That there is no practicable less intrusive alternative means of solving the anticipated problem than immediate sterilisation, in other words that (a) sterilisation is advisable at the time of the application rather than in the future, (b) the proposed method of sterilisation entails the least invasion of the Patient's body, (c) sterilisation will not itself cause physical or psychological damage greater than the intended beneficial effects, (d) the current state of scientific and medical knowledge does not suggest either (i) that a reversible sterilisation procedure or other less drastic solutions to the problem sought to be avoided, eg, some other contraceptive method, will shortly be available or (ii) that science is on the threshold of an advance in the treatment of the Patient's disability and (e) in the case of a contraceptive sterilisation all less drastic contraceptive methods, including supervision, education and training, have proved unworkable or inapplicable.

Official Solicitor
May, 1993

This note replaces the Practice Notes reported at [1989] 2 FLR 447 and [1990] 2 FLR 530

Appendix E

OFFICIAL SOLICITOR TO THE SUPREME COURT
PRACTICE NOTE ON PERSISTENT VEGETATIVE STATE

The need for the prior sanction of a High Court judge

1 The termination of artificial feeding and hydration for patients in a persistent vegetative state will in virtually all cases require the prior sanction of a High Court judge: *Airedale NHS Trust -v- Bland [1993] AC 789*[1]; *Frenchay Healthcare NHS Trust -v- S [1994]* Times 19th January.

The diagnosis

2 The Medical Ethics Committee of the British Medical Association issued guidelines on treatment decisions for patients in persistent vegetative state (PVS) in July, 1993. According to the BMA, current methods of diagnosing PVS cannot be regarded as infallible. Such a diagnosis should not be considered confirmed until the patient has been insentient for a least 12 months. Before then, as soon as the patient's condition has stabilised, rehabilitative measures such as coma arousal programmes should be instituted[2]. For a discussion of the diagnosis of PVS and of other conditions with which it is sometimes confused, see Appendix 4 (and paragraphs 156 to 162 and 251 to 258) of the Report of the House of Lords Select Committee on Medical Ethics (HL Paper 21-I: Session 1993-4: HMSO 31 January 1994).

Applications to court

3 Applications to court should be by originating summons issued in the Family Division of the High Court seeking a declaration

---

1 per Sir Stephen Brown P at p.805F (approved by the House of Lords)
2 *Airedale NHS Trust -v- Bland* per Lord Goff at p.871C

in the form set out at 4 below. Subject to specific provisions below, the application should follow the procedure laid down for sterilisation cases by the House of Lords in *Re F (Mental Patient: Sterilisation) [1990] 2 AC 1* and in the Official Solicitor's practice note dated May, 1993[3].

4 The originating summons should seek relief in the following form:

"It is declared that despite the inability of [X] to give a valid consent, the plaintiffs and/or the responsible medical practitioners:

(i) *may lawfully discontinue all life-sustaining treatment and medical support measures designed to keep [X] alive in his existing persistent vegetative state including the termination of ventilation, nutrition and hydration by artificial means and*

(ii) *may lawfully discontinue and thereafter need not furnish medical treatment to [X] except for the sole purpose of enabling [X] to end his life and to die peacefully with the greatest dignity and the least distress.*

It is ordered that in the event of a material change in the existing circumstances occurring before the withdrawal of artificial feeding and hydration any party shall have liberty to apply for such further or other declaration or order as may be just."

5 The case should normally be heard in chambers and the judgement given in open court.

The parties

6 The applicants may be either the next-of-kin or the relevant area health authority/NHS Trust (which in any event ought to be a party). The views of the next-of-kin are very important and should be made known to the court in every case.

7 The Official Solicitor should be invited to act as guardian ad litem of the patient, who will inevitably be a patient within the meaning of RSC 1965 Ord. 80.

---

3 [1993] 3 All ER 222

The evidence

8   There should be at least two neurological reports on the patient, one of which will be commissioned by the Official Solicitor. Other medical evidence, such as evidence about rehabilitation or nursing care, may be necessary.

The views of the patient

9   The views of the patient may have been previously expressed, either in writing or otherwise. The High Court exercising its inherent jurisdiction may determine the effect of a purported advance directive as to future medical treatment: In *Re T (Adult: Refusal of Treatment) [1993] Fam. 95; Re C (Refusal of Medical Treatment) [1994] 1 FLR 31.* In summary, the patient's previously expressed views, if any, will always be a very important component in the decisions of the doctors and the court.

Consultation

10 Members of the Official Solicitor's legal staff are prepared to discuss PVS cases before proceedings have been issued. Contact with the Official Solicitor may be made be telephoning 0171 911 7127 during office hours.

Official Solicitor to the Supreme Court
81 Chancery Lane
London WC2A 1DD

March, 1994

Appendix F

[Ref:]

MEDICAL CERTIFICATE
FOR THE OFFICIAL SOLICITOR TO THE SUPREME COURT

Patient's full name   Re: Mr/Mrs/Miss/Ms*...

Full name and   I   ....
address of medical
practitioner   of   ....

Medical   ....
qualifications and
office held

hereby certify as follows:

Please refer to   1. I last examined the patient on .... 19 ....
accompanying   and in my opinion the patient is capable of managing
notes   and administering his/her property and affairs.

2. Comments:

....

....

....

....

....

....

....

*Delete as
appropriate
                       Dated the. ....day of...........................19....................

7/1993
OS/MC4   Signed ....

133

[Ref:]

MEDICAL CERTIFICATE
FOR THE OFFICIAL SOLICITOR TO THE SUPREME COURT

Patient's full name   Re: Mr/Mrs/Miss/Ms*..

Full name and address of medical practitioner   I..

of ....

Medical qualifications and office held

....

hereby certify as follows:

By Section 1(2) of the Mental Health Act 1983 "mental disorder" is defined as "mental illness, arrested or incomplete development of mind, psychopathic disorder and any other disorder or disability of mind"; and "psychopathic disorder" is defined as "a persistent disorder or disability of mind (whether or not including significant impairment of intelligence) which results in abnormally aggressive or seriously irresponsible conduct on the part of the person concerned".

Please refer to accompanying notes

1. I last examined the patient on .... 19 ....
and in my opinion the patient is incapable by reason of mental disorder as defined in the Mental Health Act 1983 of managing and administering his/her property and affairs.

2. The nature of the mental disorder and the reasons for my opinion are as follows:

....

....

....

3. To the best of my knowledge and belief:

a) The present mental disorder has lasted since:

....

b) Is the patient capable of giving any rational answers to questions about legal proceedings?   Yes/No*

c) Would such questioning be harmful to him/her?   Yes/No*

d) Life expectancy and prospects of mental recovery:

....

....

....

*Delete as appropriate

7/1993
OS/MC1

Dated the.............................day of ....19 ....

Signed ....

[Ref:]

MEDICAL CERTIFICATE (ADOPTION)
FOR THE OFFICIAL SOLICITOR TO THE SUPREME COURT

Patient's full name

Re: Mr/Mrs/Miss/Ms*...

Full name and
address of medical
practitioner

I..

of ....

Medical
qualifications and
office held

....

hereby certify as follows:

By Section 1(2) of
the Mental Health
Act 1983 "mental
disorder" is defined
as "mental illness,
arrested or incom-
plete development
of mind, psycho-
pathic disorder and
any other disorder
or disability of
mind"; and "psy-
chopathic disorder"
is defined as "a per-
sistent disorder or
disability of mind
(whether or not
including signifi-
cant impairment
of intelligence)
which results in
abnormally aggres-
sive or seriously
irresponsible con-
duct on the part of
the person con-
cerned".

Please refer to
accompanying
notes

1. I last examined the patient on .... 19 ....
    and in my opinion the patient is incapable by reason of
    mental disorder as defined in the Mental Health Act 1983
    of managing and administering his/her property and
    affairs.

2. The nature of the mental disorder and the reasons for my
    opinion are as follows:

    ....

    ....

    ....

3. To the best of my knowledge and belief:

    a) The present mental disorder has lasted since:

    ....

    b) Is the patient capable of giving any rational answers
       to questions about legal proceedings?   Yes/No*

    c) Would such questioning be harmful to him/her?
                                                     Yes/No*

    d) Is the patient capable of giving agreement to adoption?
       (N.B. This means rational agreement)   Yes/No*

    e) Life expectancy and prospects of mental recovery:

    ....

    ....

    ....

*Delete as
appropriate

7/1993
OS/MC2

Dated the ....day of ....19 ....

Signed...

OFFICIAL SOLICITOR TO THE SUPREME COURT
Notes to Accompany Certificate of Incapacity

1 Doctors should be aware that if a person who is involved in legal proceedings becomes incapable by reason of mental disorder of managing his property and affairs, his interests ought to be protected by the appointment of a next friend (in the case of a plaintiff) or a guardian ad litem (in the case of a defendant) who will conduct the proceedings on his behalf. The Official Solicitor is usually approached in cases where there is no other willing and suitable candidate.

2 Before anyone may seek appointment as a next friend or guardian as litem, medical evidence must be obtained to establish that the person in question is incapable of managing and administering his property and affairs by virtue of mental disorder (as defined in Section 1 of the Mental Health Act 1983).

3 Critera for assessing incapacity are not identical with those for assessing the need for compulsory admission to hospital. The fact that a person is suffering from mental disorder within the meaning of the Mental Health Act 1983, whether living in the community or resident in hospital, detained or informal, is not of itself evidence of incapacity to manage his affairs. On the other hand, a person may be so incapable and yet not be liable to compulsory admission to hospital.

4 The certifying doctor may be either the person's general practitioner or any other registered medical practitioner who has examined the patient.

5 The Official Solicitor's certificate requires the doctor to state in paragraph 3 the grounds on which he bases his opinion of incapacity. It is this part of the certificate which appears to give the doctor the most difficulty. What is required is not merely a diagnosis (although this should be included) but a simple statement giving clear evidence of incapacity which an intelligent lay person could understand, eg. reference to defect of short-term memory, of spatial and temporal orientation or of reasoning ability, or to reckless behaviour (sometimes periodic as in mania) without regard for the future, or evidence of vulnerability to exploitation.

6 In many cases of senile dementia, severe brain damage, acute or chronic psychiatric disorder and severe mental impairment the assessment of incapacity should present little difficulty. Cases of functional and personality disorders may give more problems and assessment may depend on the individual doctor's interpretation of mental disorder. It may assist doctors to know that particularly in cases of periodic remission, the Official Solicitor will ensure that the patient's condition is regularly reassessed. In appropriate cases the Official Solicitor will take immediate steps to ensure his removal as next friend or guardian ad litem clearing the way for the individual to resume control of his affairs.

Reference in this note to the masculine should be taken to refer to the feminine where appropriate
7/1992
OS/MC3

Appendix G

NO.

COURT OF PROTECTION
MEDICAL CERTIFICATE

In the matter of

(Full name of Patient...

(please use Block Capitals)

- Please read the attached notes before completing this form.
- Please answer all questions (except where indicated) as fully as you can.
- Correct boxes should be marked with a ' ✓ '

INSTRUCTIONS Insert your full name and address	I .... of .... hereby certify as follows: 1. I have the following medical qualifications ....
Insert the Patient's present address	2. I am the medical attendant of the above-named Patient who resides at .... and have so acted since ....
For a definition of "mental disorder" see note 2 attached	3. I last examined the Patient on the ....19....... and in my opinion the Patient is incapable by reason of mental disorder of managing and administering his/her property and affairs.
State the nature of the mental disorder and the reasons for the opinion expressed. Your attention is drawn to notes 5, 6 and 7 attached **PD CP3 MM/8-95**	4. My opinion is based on the following diagnosis and the following evidence of incapacity. (1)

5. The present mental disorder has lasted since ....

6. Is the Patient a danger to himself/herself or others
   in any way? ☐Yes ☐No

   If yes, give details

7. Is the Patient capable of appreciating his/her
   surroundings? ☐Yes ☐No

   Please comment

8. Does the Patient need anything to provide
   additional comfort? ☐Yes ☐No

   If yes, what recommendations do you make?

9. Is there a reasonable prospect of the Patient:

   (a) being moved to a nursing home or residential
   home ☐Yes ☐No

   (b) returning to his /her own home if not living
   there at present ☐Yes ☐No

   If yes, when?

10. Is the Patient visited by relatives or friends? ☐Yes ☐No

   If yes:

   a) How frequently?

   b) By whom?

11. What is the Patient's age?

(2)

12. What is the Patient's life expectancy?   ☐ Under   ☐ Over
                                                  5 years   5 years

13. Please give a brief summary of the Patient's physical condition.

14. What are the Patient's prospects of mental recovery?

15. Have you or your family any financial interest in the
    accommodation in which the patient is living?   ☐Yes ☐No

16. Additional comments (if any) *(Please see note 8)*

Signed ....

Dated ....

(3)

Notes

- Please read these notes before completing the Medical Certificate.

- Please note that when the medical certificate has been completed its contents will be confidential to the Court and the Public Trustee and those authorised by the Court or the Public Trustee to see it.

- These notes have been prepared in consultation with the Royal College of Psychiatrists and the British Medical Association.

1. Doctors should be aware that if a person owning real or personal property becomes incapable, by reason of mental disorder, of safeguarding and managing his affairs, an application should be made to the Court of Protection for the appointment of a receiver or to the Public Trustee for such directions as may be necessary.

2. An application to the Court of Protection for the appointment of a receiver or to the Public Trustee for directions must be supported by a medical certificate stating that, in the doctor's opinion, the patient is incapable of managing and administering his property and affairs by virtue of mental disorder as defined in Section 1 of the Mental Health Act 1983. "Mental Disorder" is defined in Section 1(2) of the act as meaning "mental illness, arrested or incomplete development of mind, psychopathic disorder and any other disorder or disability of mind", and "psychopathic disorder" is defined as "disorder or disability of mind (whether or not including significant impairment of intelligence) which results in abnormally aggressive or seriously irresponsible conduct on the part of the person concerned".

3. Criteria for assessing incapacity are not identical with those for assessing the need for compulsory admission to hospital. The fact that a person is suffering from mental disorder within the meaning of the Mental Health Act 1983, whether living in the community or resident in hospital, detained or informal, is not of itself evidence of incapacity to manage his affairs. On the other hand, a person may be so incapable and yet not be liable to compulsory admission to hospital.

141

4. The certifying doctor may be either the person's general practitioner or any other registered medical practitioner who has examined the patient.

5. The medical certificate requires the doctor to state in paragraph 3 the nature of the mental disorder and the grounds on which he bases his opinion of incapacity. It is this part of the certificate which appears to give the doctor the most difficulty. What is required is a diagnosis and a simple statement giving clear evidence of incapacity which an intelligent lay person could understand, eg. reference to defect of short-term memory, of spatial and temporal orientation or of reasoning ability, or to reckless spending (sometimes periodic as in mania) without regard for the future, or evidence of vulnerability to exploitation.

6. In many cases of senile dementia, severe brain damage, acute or chronic psychiatric disorder and severe mental impairment the assessment of incapacity should present little difficulty. Cases of functional and personality disorders may give more problems and assessment may depend on the individual doctor's interpretation of mental disorder. The Court and the Public Trustee tend towards the view that these conditions render a person liable to their jurisdiction where there appears to be a real danger that they will lead to dissipation of considerable capital assets.

7. A person may not be dealt with under the Mental Health Act 1983, and may not be the subject of an application to the Court of Protection or the Public Trustee, by reason only of promiscuity or other immoral conduct, sexual deviance or dependence on alcohol or drugs.

8. The Court and the Public Trustee attach considerable importance to receipt by the patient of notice of the proposed proceedings, since the patient may have an objection, though irrational, to the appointment of a particular person or may, even unwittingly, contribute information of assistance to the Court or the Public Trustee. The Court and Public Trustee are reluctant to exercise their power to dispense with notification, unless it could be injurious to the patient's health, because it is considered that a person has a right to know – or at least be

given an opportunity to understand – if the management of his affairs is to be taken out of his hands and thereafter dealt with by someone on his behalf; if he has no understanding at all, then notification cannot affect him adversely, and a patient who has sufficient insight to appreciate the significance of the proceedings may need reassurance that they are for his benefit. If the certifying doctor believes that, in a particular case, notification of the proceedings by or under the supervision of the doctor is advisable, he should say so when completing the form **CP3**.

9.   The grounds for dispensing with the need for notice being served are:-

(a) the patient is incapable of understanding it, or

(b) such notification would be injurious to the patient's health, or

(c) for any other reason notification ought to be dispensed with.

10.   The completed medical certificate should be returned to either the solicitors in the matter or to **The Public Trust Office, Protection Division, Stewart House, 24 Kingsway, London WC2B 6JX.**

Further Reading

Law Society Publications

Ashton G R, *The Elderly Client Handbook - The Law Society's Guide to Acting for Older People*, 1994, The Law Society

The Guide to the Professional Conduct of Solicitors, 6th Edn, 1993, The Law Society

British Medical Association Publications

Advance Statements About Medical Treatment, 1995, BMA

The Older Person: Consent and Care, 1995, BMA

Medical Ethics Today: Its Practice and Philosophy, 1993, BMA

Rights and Responsibilities of Doctors, 1992, BMA

Law Commission Publications

Law Commission *Consultation Paper 119, Mentally Incapacitated Adults and Decision Making: An Overview*, 1991, HMSO

Law Commission *Consultation Paper 128, Mentally Incapacitated Adults and Decision Making: A New Jurisdiction*, 1993, HMSO

Law Commission *Consultation Paper 129, Mentally Incapacitated Adults and Decision Making: Medical Treatment and Research*, 1993, HMSO

Law Commission *Consultation Paper 130, Mentally Incapacitated Adults and Other Vulnerable Adults: Public Law Protection*, 1993, HMSO

Law Commission *Report 231, Mental Incapacity*, 1995, HMSO

Other Relevant Publications

Law relating to mental incapacity

Ashton G R, *Elderly People and the Law*, 1995, Butterworths

Ashton G R, *Mental Handicap and the Law*, 1992, Sweet & Maxwell

Department of Health and Welsh Office *Code of Practice: Mental Health Act 1983*, 2nd Edn, 1993, HMSO

Gostin L, *Mental Health Services - Law and Practice* (looseleaf), Shaw & Son

Hoggett B, *Mental Health Law*, 1990, Sweet & Maxwell

Jones R, *Mental Health Act Manual*, 4th Edn, 1994, Sweet & Maxwell

Medical treatment

Brazier M, *Medicine, Patients and the Law*, 2nd Edn, 1992, Penguin Books

Kennedy I, & Grubb A, *Medical Law: Text with Materials*, 1994, Butterworths

Mason J K, & McCall Smith A, *Law and Medical Ethics*, 4th Edn, 1994, Butterworths

Financial management

Cretney S, *Enduring Powers of Attorney - A Practitioner's Guide*, 1991, Family Law

Letts P, *Managing Other People's Money*, 1990, Age Concern England

Whitehorn N, *Heywood & Massey Court of Protection Practice*, 12th Edn, 1991, Sweet & Maxwell

Whitehorn N, *Court of Protection Handbook*, 1988, Longman

Inheritance

Butterworths *Wills, Probate and Administration Services* (looseleaf), Butterworths

Index